LANGUAGE ACQUISITION AND SYNTACTIC THEORY

STUDIES IN THEORETICAL PSYCHOLINGUISTICS

VOLUME 14

The titles published in this series are listed at the end of this volume.

AMY E. PIERCE

LANGUAGE ACQUISITION AND SYNTACTIC THEORY

A Comparative Analysis of French and English Child Grammars

KLUWER ACADEMIC PUBLISHERS

DORDRECHT / BOSTON / LONDON

Library of Congress Cataloging-in-publication Data

Pierce, Amy E.
    Language acquisition and syntactic theory : a comparative analysis
of French and English child grammars / Amy E. Pierce.
        p.   cm. -- (Studies in theoretical psycholinguistics ; v. 14)
    Revision of author's thesis (doctoral--1989).
    "October, 1991."
    Includes bibliographical references and index.
    ISBN 0-7923-1553-7 (acid free paper)
    1. Language acquisition. 2. Grammar, Comparative and general-
-Syntax. 3. French language--Grammar, Comparative--English.
4. English language--Grammar, Comparative--French.   I. Title.
II. Series.
P118.P49 1992
401'.93--dc20   91-38522

ISBN 0-7923-1553-7

Published by Kluwer Academic Publishers,
P.O.Box 17, 3300 AA Dordrecht, The Netherlands

Kluwer Academic Publishers incorporates the publishing programmes
of D. Reidel, Martinus Nijhoff, Dr W. Junk and MTP Press.

Sold and distributed in the U.S.A. and Canada
by Kluwer Academic Publishers,
101 Philip Drive, Norwell, MA 02061, U.S.A.

In all other countries, sold and distributed
by Kluwer Academic Publishers Group,
P.O. Box 322, 3300 AH Dordrecht, The Netherlands.

Printed on acid-free paper

Printed in the Netherlands.

To Eldar

TABLE OF CONTENTS

ACKNOWLEDGMENTS

This book is based upon my dissertation (Pierce, 1989). Thanks foremost to Ken Wexler, who chaired my doctoral committee and has been a tremendous source of advice and encouragement throughout. Thanks also to Tom Roeper and two anonymous reviewers for their helpful comments. And to all those who know they are owed thanks – colleagues, many friends, immediate and extended family – for their input, warmth and support.

CHAPTER 1

LANGUAGE ACQUISITION AND SYNTACTIC THEORY

1.1 INTRODUCTION

It is obvious even to the untrained observer that the mastery of spoken language proceeds without much strain on the part of the child, and without explicit instruction. Research on linguistic development has established that the human infant is indeed predisposed to learn language. Language and language growth, however, are not typically amenable to study in the biological laboratory. It is largely by unearthing uniformities in the stages of language development, across children and across languages, that the acquisition theorist contributes to the discovery of the mind's blueprints for language. This book considers data from French and English child language, focusing on the interplay between syntactic theory and language acquisition. French and English are, according to certain measures, grammatically similar. For instance, both are configurational head-first languages, with syntactic wh-movement and a relatively impoverished system for marking subject-verb agreement in the simple present tense. But there are recognized distinctions between the two grammatical systems, and the acquisition facts I present highlight these as well as other, unexpected differences.

My central claim is that a large cluster of phenomena in linguistic development are largely explained by a single, independently motivated hypothesis concerning the grammar. Namely, I assume, following a number of proposals in the recent syntactic literature, that the subject of a sentence is generated internal to the verb phrase, rather than outside the verb phrase in what was commonly thought to be the base position of the subject (Kuroda, 1896; Kitagawa, 1986; Contreras, 1987 Fukui and Speas, 1987; Sportiche, 1988). On the basis of the VP-internal subject theory and a few auxiliary assumptions, also independently motivated, fundamental patterns in the crosslinguistic acquisition of word order, verbal inflection and negation, as well as the well-known phenomenon of null subjects in early language, are accounted for. Each of these domains of syntactic development is characterized, if you will, by an acquisition puzzle:

Word order. Although French and English are generally thought to be equivalent with respect to the underlying linear order of constituents and a lack of free inversion of the subject, there are striking differences between French and English child language in the domain of word order. While children acquiring English are known to depart from accepted sentential word order only rarely (Brown, 1973; Pinker, 1984), French two year-olds produce subject-final constructions in abundance (Lightbown, 1977; Clark, 1985). This salient difference between French and English child language has remained largely unexplored.

Inflectional affixation. Very early child language is characterized by the absence of inflectional morphology, yet there is the following developmental paradox. The English speaking child is slow to acquire the impoverished inflectional system of his language, more often than not leaving out grammatical morphemes and auxiliary verbs until about the age of three (e.g. Brown, 1973). Yet the Italian speaking child, for example, is relatively quick to learn the complex system of inflectional morphology in his language, achieving productivity in this domain before the age of two (e.g. Bates, 1976; Hyams, 1984). Since intuitive notions of complexity fail to capture the developmental facts, what notion of complexity is relevant to the acquisition of inflectional morphology in English and French?

Negation. The early negated sentences of English speaking children contain negation on the left periphery of the sentence, sometimes with an overt subject below the negative marker (e.g. *No I see truck*; *No Mommy giving baby Sarah milk*) (Klima and Bellugi, 1966; Bellugi, 1967). The result is a construction that is never attested in the adult language which serves as input to the child. What leads the English speaking child to produce these novel constructions? For that matter, what leads the young French speaking child to produce similarly ungrammatical negatives, though to a lesser degree?

Null subjects. The phenomenon of subject omission in child language stands out as one of the most robust cases of an acquisition universal. As far as we know, no matter what language a two year-old may be learning, he will appear to treat the subject of sentences as omissible. Of course, null subjects are expected from the child learning a language, such as Spanish, in which null subjects are grammatical, as is the case in the majority of the world's languages (Gilligan, 1987). In contrast, overt subjects are assumed to be required by the grammars of English and French. Nonetheless, children acquiring these languages omit lexical subjects with striking regularity.

In what follows, I substantiate each of these phenomena with natural production data from French and English child language, and provide an account in terms of a grammatical framework which includes the VP-internal subject hypothesis. According to this framework, and perhaps as its defining characteristic, inflectional structure and basic clausal structure (i.e. the verb and its arguments) are divorced in underlying syntactic representation. Syntactic derivational processes which integrate them by moving the subject, the verb and the elements of inflection are subject to parameter setting and, in certain cases, may only be acquired after an interim of delay. In particular, I build evidence for the hypothesis that early language has VP-internal subjects unmoved. From this follows a variety of word order distinctions between child and adult language, including subject-final order in early French, auxiliary-initial order in early English and negation-initial order, to varying degrees, in the youngest sentential output of both. In addition, null subjects in French and English child language can be explained on the assumption that Infl counts as a governor and Case assigner in early grammar, licensing *pro* in VP-internal subject position when directional government holds (Adams, 1987).

In constructing this model of early grammar, I further assume that the affixation of verbal inflection is a syntactic process which takes different forms in French and English. While verbs raise to Infl in the syntax of French, affixes lower into the VP in the syntax of English (Emonds, 1978; Chomsky, 1988; Pollock, 1989). With the exception of *be* and auxiliary *have*, there is no verb-to-Infl movement in Modern English. Verb raising is one way in which verb-subject order in early French appears to be derived. The absence of verb-raising in English is visible in the generation of negation-initial and auxiliary-initial constructions in early speech. The failure of subjects to raise out of the VP in early grammar is in part attributable to the initial hypothesis, based on a default parameter setting, concerning the structural assignment of nominative Case.

I contend in the pages to come, therefore, that crosslinguistic data from child language converge to provide impressive confirmation of the VP-internal subject hypothesis. These data also conform to the proposed distinction between English and French in terms of inflectional-derivational processes, as well as the principled bias in Universal Grammar (UG) toward minimal (in some well-defined sense) syntactic derivations. The overall picture to emerge from these studies is that verbal inflection and the verb phrase, containing the subject, are divorced at an initial stage in S-structural representation, just as they are in the underlying syntactic structure. This is readily construed within the theoretical framework as a small window of delay in the acquisition of the derivational process of subject raising to [Spec, IP] in contexts where it is obligatory in the adult grammar. I argue in this way against recent suggestions in the acquisition literature to the effect that functional categories including Infl are absent in early child language (Guilfoyle and Noonan, 1988; Aldridge, 1988, Radford, 1990), and similarly against the claim that the Case filter or the Case module is not functional at early stages of child language (Lebeaux, 1988; Bloom, 1988). Finally, the success of this framework in accounting for aspects of syntax acquisition lends further credibility to recent enrichments of linguistic theory. I turn now to a more detailed description of these theoretical proposals.

1.2 THEORETICAL BACKGROUND

In this section, I provide some background for the studies of child language presented in chapters 2 through 6. Specifically, I outline the VP-internal subject theory, the verb raising analysis of inflectional affixation in French, and the affix lowering analysis of inflectional affixation in English (Emonds, 1976; Chomsky, 1988; Pollock, 1989). Furthermore, I bring together a group of proposals, which seemingly arose independently in the acquisition and syntactic literature, to the effect that UG is biased toward minimal derivations (Hyams, 1986a; Kitagawa, 1986; Chomsky, 1988; Borer and Wexler, 1988). These proposals conspire to suggest a rudimentary metric of grammatical complexity which constrains the course of acquisition. I assume the theory of grammatical principles and parameters set out in Chomsky (1981) and enriched in much subsequent work, including Chomsky (1986a,b;1988) as well as published and unpublished work by numerous others. I do not undertake a review of the fundamental postulates of the theory, as I am primarily concerned with the application of a few recent proposals to findings in child language. I will therefore outline only the theoretical apparatus particularly relevant to the present discussion.

1.2.1 The VP-internal subject hypothesis

A number of proposals in the syntactic literature of recent years converge on the following theme: the sentential subject in French- and English-type languages is generated within the maximal projection of the verb as the sister of an intermediate projection of the verb (Kitagawa, 1986; Contreras, 1987; Fukui, 1988; Sportiche, 1988; Koopman and Sportiche, 1988, among others). According to this hypothesis, the D-structure representation of the sentence in (1) is as in (2):

(1)   The cat will eat the flower

(2)

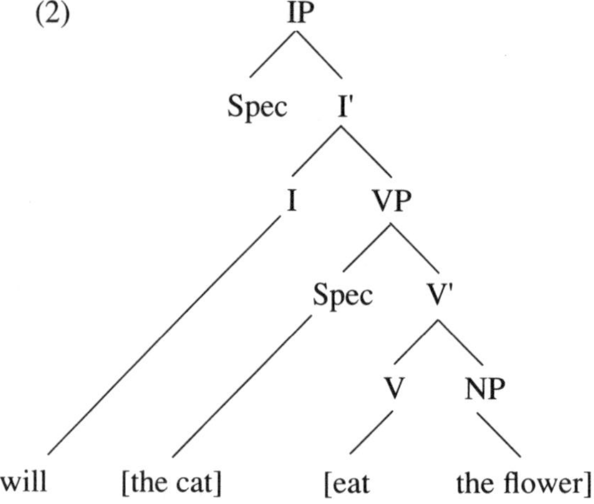

On this theory, subjects, like objects, are theta marked within the maximal projection of the verb. Generalizing over the various approaches, it is argued that subjects in English and French fail to be assigned nominative Case in the VP-internal specifier position. They must raise via move-alpha to another position, specifier of IP, where nominative Case can be assigned under Spec-Head agreement, rather than structurally. In contrast, subjects within the VP in certain other languages, for instance Spanish, may be assigned Case directly within the VP and are thus licensed to remain there. The proposals differ on the question of how constituents within the VP are ordered. According to Sportiche (1988) and Koopman and Sportiche (1988), the order of constituents within the English VP is S-V-O, as in (2). Since these authors argue that the order of constituents within the VP is not determined by X-bar theory or theta theory, presumably the underlying rigid word order of English is the result of a parametric choice specifying linear order.

According to Kitagawa (1986), on the other hand, the subject in English is generated as the right branching sister of V'. That is, English has an underlying word order of V-O-S, as in (3), where raising of the subject results in S-V-O word order at S-structure:

(3)

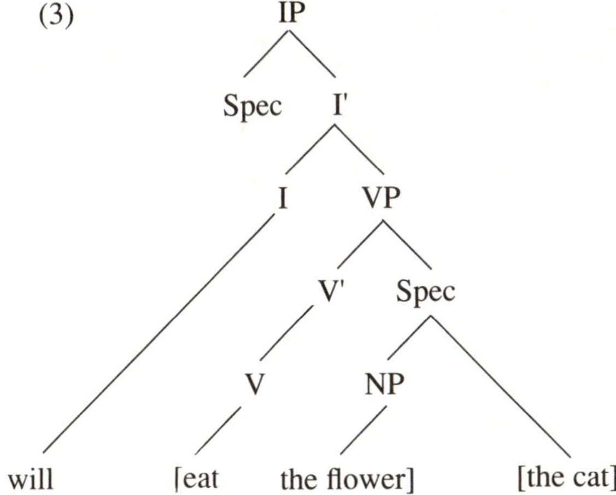

In Kitagawa's model, the subject-final property of underlying structure is critical on two counts. First, it accomplishes uni-directional head government of internal and external arguments, which has been argued for on independent grounds (e.g. Stowell, 1983; Travis, 1984). Second, Kitagawa's model is motivated to account for cases of extraposition in English, which conform directly to V-O-S order. For example, the sentence in (4) is analyzed on this approach as being a direct realization of the base V-O-S structure, with the pleonastic *it* base generated in [Spec, IP] and the sentential subject generated in [Spec, VP][1],[2]

(4)   It [$_{VP}$ bothers me [$_{spec}$ that he hasn't called us yet]]

In Contreras' (1987) account, simple sentences in English are portrayed as involving no subject raising, given affix lowering and underlying S-V order within the English VP. Furthermore, Spanish is claimed to have the option to generate the subject either to the right or to the left of the verb. Because the subject can be assigned Case in either position in Spanish on this account, the occurrence of both subject-verb and verb-subject word orders in Spanish is readily explained. Both orders are underived, in the sense that no constituent need move.[3] As mentioned, Sportiche (1988) also maintains that the position of the subject within the VP is variable, but "only in languages that exhibit both orders overtly" (p. 445). Stylistic inversion in French is taken as evidence that in those languages the ordering of the subject and the verb within the VP is not fixed, while in English it is.

Borer (1986a), although not arguing that all subjects are generated within the VP, accounts for postverbal subjects in Italian along the same lines. That is, she suggests that postverbal subjects are base generated, right branching sisters to a projection of the verb, as in (3). On Borer's account, the verbal projection assigns an external theta role directly to the subject in this position. Assuming that nominative Case is assigned under government by agreement (AGR) (Chomsky, 1981), and that AGR is lowered onto the verb in the syntax, then nominative Case can be assigned directly to the postverbal subject. In Borer's model, the preverbal subject position [Spec, IP] need not even be generated under these conditions, since Case assignment to the postverbal subject is accomplished without the formation of a chain.

Of these authors, Contreras (1987) makes what are perhaps the most radical claims about the structure of the simple English sentence. His approach figures importantly in my account of the acquisition of English word order, and in further speculations about the relationship between acquisition and language change. As for how nominative Case might be assigned to the VP-internal subject in child grammars, I assume that Infl canonically governs and assigns nominative Case to the VP-internal subject. Koopman and Sportiche (1988) propose a parameter according to which Infl is either an optional or obligatory subject raising category. In optional subject raising languages, both overt and empty VP-internal subjects are licensed under government by Infl. In an obligatory subject raising language like English, on the other hand, nominative Case is assigned as a rule under Spec-Head agreement, not under government. According to Koopman and Sportiche, then, the underlying VP-internal subject structure conforms to the configuration for nominative Case assignment in languages without obligatory subject raising. In their framework and elsewhere, Infl can head-govern the maximal projection of the verb and its specifier and thereby assign Case to the VP-internal subject (Deprez, 1988; Bonet, 1989). When nominative Case is assigned under government, the subject is not forced to raise.

1.2.2 *Inflectional affixation in French and English*

In both the French and English systems, inflectional affixiation is a syntactic process.[4] That is, the attachment of tense and agreement affixes takes place in the syntax, rather than as part of derivational morphology (cf. Emonds, 1985). Following Emonds (1978; 1985), Chomsky (1988) and Pollock (1989), I assume that inflectional affixation is accomplished differently in French and English. According to these authors, the verb in French raises to Infl to pick up its tense and agreement morphology. In English, main verbs do not raise to Infl. Rather, inflection lowers into the verb phrase; only *be* and the auxiliary *have* undergo raising in syntax.

This formal distinction between English and French is substantiated by, among other things, the placement of negation and adverbs with respect to the verb. In French, the inflected verb regularly occurs to the left of the negative particle *pas* and VP adverbs. While auxiliary verbs in English pattern with French verbs in this respect, main verbs in English occur to the right of negation and VP adverbs:

(5)   a. Le chat chasse *souvent* les oiseaux.
        b. The cat *often* chases the birds.

(6)   a. Le chat (ne) chasse *pas* le chien.
        b. The cat does *not* chase the dog.

Assuming that the adverb is situated within the VP and that its position is fixed, examples such as (5a) indicate that the French verb has moved to some position on the left of the VP. Similarly, assuming that the position of negative *pas* within inflection is fixed, examples like (6a) show that the French verb has raised to a position above negation within the inflectional complex.

Another difference between the inflectional systems of English and French that figures in my discussion of the comparative child language data is the fact that only English has a set of modal auxiliaries that are generated within inflection. Modal verbs in French are generated in VP and raise like other main verbs. While tense and agreement in French are always instantiated as inflectional affixes, English can realize tensed inflection in the form of a base-generated modal. This leads to an interesting class of word order errors in English child language, described in chapter 4, errors which do not arise in the acquisition of French.

Finally, I adopt the proposal that tense and agreement head separate projections, contributing to a highly detailed representation of the inflectional complex (Chomsky, 1988; Pollock, 1989). In the most articulated version of this proposal, there are two agreement projections, one below the projection of tense and one above it (Chomsky, 1988). The lower AGR functions in recent analyses of participle agreement in Romance (cf. Kayne, 1987), and of raising of nonfinite verb forms (Deprez, 1988; Pollock, 1989). The higher AGR governs and assigns nominative Case to the subject in [Spec, IP] position. I also assume the presence of a projection of negation. Following Pollock (1989), Zanuttini (1989) and others, I take it that *pas* is the French counterpart of English *not*, rendered as *no* in the speech of some young children. As in English, the French marker of negation occurs below the projection of Infl and above the VP. Accordingly, the basic negative structure for English and French is as portrayed in (7):

(7)   English/French negation

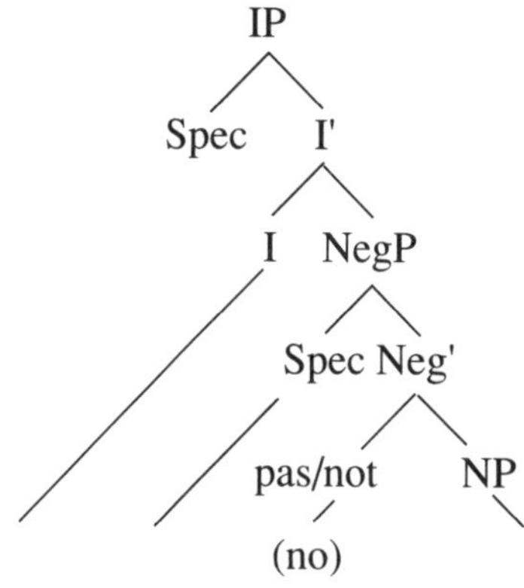

1.2.3 The economy of derivation framework

In contemporary syntactic theory, considerations of acquisition go hand-in-hand with considerations of crosslinguistic viability of the theory. The parameters that constrain structural variation among languages also constrain theories of syntactic acquisition. Specific conditions on derivations that have been proposed recently, particularly in the writings of Chomsky (1986b; 1988), are clearly formulated with the language learner in mind. One prime example is the vacuous movement hypothesis, discussed in Chomsky (1986b). This principle states that vacuous movement, as in the case of wh-subject questions (e.g. *Who chases birds?*), is not obligatory at S-structure, although it is at the level of logical form. The justification for this hypothesis is that "the language learner assumes that there is syntactic movement only where there is overt evidence for it" (Chomsky, 1986b, p. 50), where presumably "overt evidence" refers to permutations in word order.

In a similar vein, Chomsky (1988) proposes a set of least effort guidelines. Taken as a UG condition on derivations, the principle of least effort insures that syntactic derivations are minimal in cost, where cost is defined, at first approximation, in terms of number of steps in a derivation and, in more subtle terms, as the extent to which language specific principles are invoked in a derivation.

... the "least effort" condition must be interpreted so that UG principles are applied wherever possible, with language-particular rules used only to "save" a D-structure yielding no output ... UG principles are thus "less costly" than language-specific principles. We may think of them, intuitively, as "wired-in" and distinguished from the acquired elements of language, which bear a greater cost. (Chomsky, 1988, p. 9)

Chomsky (1988) employs the least effort condition in arguing that verb raising to Infl, for the purpose of affixing inflectional morphology, is necessary where possible, and preferred in the relevant sense to the process of affix lowering. Verb raising is a one-step process, while affix lowering is a two-step process in that it yields an improper chain, necessitating movement of the stem+affix constituent to Infl at LF (hence, the second step). An example of a subtler notion of derivational cost is found in the explanation for why *do*-insertion in unemphatic declarative sentences (e.g. **The cat did chase the dog*) is ruled out. Supposing that *do*-insertion is a language particular rule, as seems to be the case, it may be used only as a last resort to recover an illegitimate derivation. If fails to apply otherwise.

Conditions similar to the economy of derivation have appeared elsewhere in the recent literature. Kitagawa (1986), for example, proposes an isomorphy constraint, which "permits the application of Move-alpha if and only if principles of grammar...require it" (p. 244). Hyams (1986a) proposes a similar principle that defines grammatical simplicity in terms of a high degree of isomorphism between the various levels of grammatical representation. She suggests, furthermore, that an initial parameter setting is always the one which yields the simplest grammar defined in these terms. An analogous idea has surfaced in discussions of syntactic maturation. According to Borer and Wexler (1988), the early grammar is characterized by bi-uniqueness, where maturation entails "a gradual reformulation of bi-unique relations" (p. 33). One form that bi-uniqueness takes in Borer and Wexler's model is an inability on the part of the early grammar to carry out nonlocal assignment of grammatical features (Borer and Wexler, 1987). The absence of the periphrastic passive in early English and Hebrew child language, for example, is attributed to the absence of A-chains from early grammatical representation.

These are some of the precedents for extending the least effort condition to, and testing it against, language acquisition phenomena. If this condition is in fact a principle of UG, then it follows that the child knows it, i.e. that it is hard-wired. The child, like the adult, will assume the shortest derivations licensed by his grammar, the shortest derivation in the extreme case being no derivation. The example of the vacuous movement hypothesis is relevant in this regard. Another motivation for reinterpreting the economy of derivation guidelines in acquisition-theoretic terms — in particular, the notion of cost that relates to language-specific rules — concerns the analogous distinction between core and peripheral systems (Chomsky, 1981; 1986a). Core grammar is generally understood as the sum of the principles and parameters of UG, as apart from peripheral linguistic phenomena which constitute marked exceptions to or relaxations of the conditions of core grammar. Core and peripheral systems are predicted to develop in different ways (Chomsky, 1981). In particular, the parameter setting mechanisms of language acquisition by definition constrain the core and not the periphery.

Hyams (1986b) invokes this distinction to explain certain crosslinguistic findings in the development of inflectional affixation. She observes that, while English speaking children are slow to acquire the limited inflectional morphology of their language, Italian speaking children are quick to learn the complex system of inflectional affixation in their language. This acquisition paradox was mentioned above. Clearly, intuitive notions of complexity fail to capture the developmental facts. Rather, Hyams argues, the relevant notion defines complexity in terms of deviation from the core grammatical system. The elaborate, highly visible system of inflectional morphology in Italian plants inflection firmly in the core grammar of Italian, while the impoverished system of agreement morphology in English, and in particular the fact that a verbal stem constitutes a well-formed word, relegates inflection to the periphery of English grammar. Given Hyams' theoretical metric of complexity, according to which core mechanisms are acquired prior to marked or peripheral ones, the late acquisition of inflectional morphology in English relative to Italian is explained.

Late acquisition of inflectional affixation, then, is successfully predicted on two derivationally motivated accounts. As Hyams (1986b) shows, the core-periphery distinction can account for this delay. Following Chomsky (1988), this delay is also predicted according to the relative number of derivational steps; while verb raising to Infl in Romance involves only one step, affix lowering to the verb in English involves two. The intuitive idea is that the grammar is innately biased toward derivational minimalism, defined by Chomsky (1988) and others in terms of derivation both from UG and from D-structure. The child's initial assumption is that move-alpha does not apply. He relaxes this bias only in the face of overt or salient evidence of movement, as he acquires lexical items which trigger movement, as the acquisition of one derivational process necessitates another, or perhaps as he matures. In present work, a UG bias toward derivational economy is related to the D-structure quality of child language and, in particular, to the preservation of the underlying position of the subject in early language.

This book may prove unsatisfying for those seeking general discussion about learning, or a general theory of language acquisition. My goals are more modest. Rather than amassing evidence for one conception of learning (i.e. as maturation, as overcoming performance limitations, as lexicon building), I present evidence for a parameterized grammar in the form of errors children make and those they do not make. In this way, I aim to show where the predictions of specific hypotheses concerning grammatical principles and parameters are borne out in the child language data. The intention of this book, therefore, is not to argue for one approach to language development over another. Instead, its purpose is to show that certain systematic errors that children make, especially when compared to the ones they do not make, provide evidence for a particular model of the parameterized grammar.

The theoretical assumptions outlined above give rise to a central prediction about the comparative course of grammatical development in English and French. Specifically, with respect to word order and negation, the prediction for English (where there is no raising of main verbs) is that Neg-(subject)-verb constructions will be produced at an early stage, as long as the subject fails to raise out of the VP. For French, as long as verbs raise and subjects do not, finite verb-Neg-(subject) order will surface in the young child's output. From the preceding discussion, it should be apparent that there are actually two ways to represent verb-subject order in early French language. Given verb raising to Infl, V-S order might result from underlying S-V order in conjunction with the leftward movement of the verb. Alternatively, V-S order might be a direct manifestation of underlying order, as one of two possible underived orders in French (Sportiche, 1988). Although the French child data document the existence of VP-internal subjects, due to certain ambiguities in the theory and among French verbal forms, they do not decide between these two hypotheses.

The rest of the book is organized as follows. Chapter 2 describes comparative findings in the acquisition of basic word order, confirming the VP-internal subject approach. Chapter 3 focuses on early divergent patterns in the French and English child's use of negation. Chapter 4 looks at the acquisition of inflectional affixation, supporting the view that there is a parametric distinction between English and French which leads to main verb raising in the case of French only. Chapter 5 uncovers surprisingly divergent patterns in the distribution of subject pronouns in French and English children's productions, surface differences which clearly point to differences in underlying representation. Chapter 6 is concerned with the null subject property of early language, and with showing that not all main clause null subjects are alike. Chapter 7 speculates on the relationship between language change and acquisition in the various syntactic domains. Finally, chapter 8 provides a brief look at comparative data from the acquisition of Spanish.

1.3 A METHODOLOGICAL NOTE

The speech of four children from each of the two language groups was studied.[5] The data sources, child pseudonyms, focal age-ranges and the total number of utterances considered for the French speaking children are given in (8) and, for the English speaking children, in (9):

(8) French data sources

NAME	SOURCE	AGE-RANGE	TOTAL UTTERANCES
Daniel	(Lightbown, 1977)	1–8–1 to 1–11–1	782
Grégoire	(Champaud, 1988)	1–9–2 to 2–3–0	587
Nathalie	(Lightbown, 1977)	1–9–3 to 2–3–2	592
Philippe	(Suppes et al., 1973)	2–1–3 to 2–3–0	625

(9) English data sources

NAME	SOURCE	AGE-RANGE	TOTAL UTTERANCES
Eve	(Brown, 1973)	1–6–0 to 2–0–2	1741
Naomi	(Sachs, 1983)	1–9–1 to 2–2–0	3301
Peter	(Bloom, 1970)	1–11–2 to 2–3–3	1556
Nina	(Suppes et al, 1973)	1–11–2 to 2–2–1	2553

Data for six of the eight children was accessed through the Child Language Data Exchange System (MacWhinney & Snow, 1985). The exceptions are Daniel and Nathalie, whose transcripts were made available to me by Dr. Patsy Lightbown.[6] In all cases, transcripts consist of spontaneous speech of the child in dialogue with his or her parent(s) and, on occasion, other adults. Depending upon the child, speech samples were taken at roughly one week to one month intervals. Note in (8) and (9) that ages are given, as they will continue to be throughout, in the form of years-months-weeks. I began analysis of most children's speech at the youngest available transcript, the exceptions being Naomi and Peter, whose earliest transcripts contained few decipherable verb-containing productions. In performing the calculations that I report in these pages, every effort was made to consider only and all verb-containing, affirmative, nonimperative, nonimitative utterances of the child. Often, this involved relying on the discourse context implicit in the child's exchanges with adults, as well as on any notation provided by the transcriber. Due to the uncertainty of this general method, the results reported here are subject to an undetermined (hopefully minimal) amount of coding error, some of it beyond my control.

NOTES

[1] This example is from Kitagawa, 1986, p. 239.

[2] An obvious question is what rules out other non-applications of subject raising, as in *It will eat the flower the cat*? Kitagawa argues that the Case filter rules out such cases on the assumption that the verb does not normally assign Case to internal subjects.

[3] Contreras assumes that inflectional affixation is accomplished via affix lowering in Spanish and English, entailing that the verb does not raise to Infl.

[4] Chomsky (1981) formalizes affix lowering in English as applying post-syntactically, at phonological form, in contrast to the position assumed here.

[5] Four boys and four girls were included in the study, but they are not equally divided between the two language groups.

[6] I owe much to Dr. Lightbown's generosity. The research that this book is based upon was immeasurably enhanced by the data she collected and so kindly made available to me.

CHAPTER 2

WORD ORDER

This chapter takes a first look at the comparative French-English acquisition data, examining word order in the two child languages. French and English are traditionally considered to be equivalent with respect to word order in simple declarative sentences. However, there is certainly more pronounced colloquial variability in French than in English in this respect. And, as will be discussed here, there are clearcut differences between the two languages when it comes to acquisition of basic word order. In effect, the predictions of the model for the acquisition of word order in the two languages, as sketched in the previous chapter, appear to be verified. The child acquiring English sticks to SVO with one noteworthy exception. The French child produces VS and VOS structures in abundance, and appears to prefer postverbal subjects to preverbal lexical subjects during an early and enduring phase. This remarkable fact has not previously been explored in any depth. The divergent developmental patterns are shown here to fall out from the VP-internal subject hypothesis, in conjunction with the fact that French has verb raising and English does not. I turn first to English child language.

2.1 WORD ORDER IN THE EARLY GRAMMAR OF ENGLISH

2.1.1 Background

In a study of one two-year old child, Gruber (1967) reports finding an equal number of NP subjects to the right as to the left of the predicate. This leads him to propose that the child's sentences are best described as topic-comment structures rather than as subject-predicate structures. Since most of the child's utterances at this time contain either a null subject or a pronominal subject, the number of full NP subjects in either pre- or post-predicate position is rather small. In (1) is a list of the all the utterances which Gruber labels as *topic after the comment*:

(1)   Exhaustive list of post predicate subjects from one two-year old child (Gruber, 1967)

    a. go truck
    b. go in there train
    c. go way wheels
    d. all broken wheel
    e. break pumpkin
    f. over there train
    g. in there wheels
    h. in there baby
    i. there's the man
    j. there's the truck
    k. there's the wheel

In seeming contrast to Gruber's exceptional finding of variable word order, it is generally agreed that children learning English make almost no errors in the area of basic word order. Brown (1973) writes that there are "trifling few" violations of normal word order in early English. That instances of postverbal subjects in the English child data are vanishingly rare has sometimes been attributed to conservatism in learning. In other words, the child is said to stop short of overgeneralizing from subject-auxiliary inversion in questions to errorful cases of inversion involving non auxiliary verbs (Pinker, 1984). Pinker (1984) observes only three examples of postverbal subjects in the child language data based on a review the literature and examination of thousands of utterances, and they all contain the verb *go*:

(2)   Three instances of errorful inversion in child language (Pinker, 1984)

    a. goes paci (fier) in mouth?
    b. where's going to be the school?
    c. where goes the wheel?

By looking at the data in (1) and (2), the reader will note a clear pattern. There are only two verbs occurring in the instances of word order error in (la-e) and (2). They are *go* and *break*. And the only other verb exemplified is main verb *be*, which occurs in (li-k) with the non-argument constituent *there*. The latter are grammatical: the word *there*, whether in its adverbial-locational or pleonastic role, serves to introduce sentences in which the verb precedes the subject. In other words, according to Stowell (1978) and, more recently, Burzio (1986), *be* is a raising verb. What do *go*, *break* and *be*, then, have in common? They fall into the class of verbs which do not assign a subject theta-role or accusative Case. The explanation for the pattern observed in (1) and (2) therefore plausibly lies in the nature of unaccusative verbs.

2.1.2 *Unaccusative verbs*

Intransitive verbs have been analyzed as falling into two classes, the unaccusatives and the unergatives (cf., among others, Perlmutter, 1978; Zubizarreta, 1985; Burzio, 1986; Grimshaw, 1987; Belletti, 1988). Unergatives assign only an external theta role, and are generally characterized as being agentive. These include verbs such as *talk*, *shout*, *hide*, *hate*, *pretend*, *think*, *wish*. Unaccusatives assign only an internal theta role, and are generally characterized as being nonagentive, as the unique argument is a patient. These include the verbs *come*, *go*, *arrive*, *remain*, *descend*, *climb*, *run*. Some verbs, such as *break*, *sink*, undergo transitive-unaccusative alternation:

(3)   a. Maria broke the vase/The vase broke
       b. A storm sank the boat/The boat sank

The underlying structure of English sentences containing unaccusative verbs is with the sole argument NP in direct object position:

(4)   a. D-structure: *e* arrived a woman
       b. S-structure: a woman$_1$ arrived t$_1$

The Case Filter drives movement of the object to subject position in (4b): since the unaccusative does not assign accusative Case, the NP must move to a Case-assigning position. (5) represents another way for the NP to receive Case, via coindexing with a pleonastic element base generated in subject position (Burzio, 1986):

(5)   There$_1$ arrived a woman$_1$

Like unaccusatives, *be* and other raising verbs (such as *seem*) fail to assign a subject theta role or accusative Case. They therefore also participate in the type of derivation shown in (4) and the type of coindexing shown in (5).

Given the underlying structure of the utterances in (1) and (2), they do not constitute errorful inversion. Rather, they reflect a failure to raise the NP out of it's D-structure object position.[1] In order to substantiate this analysis, we now take a closer look at the word order errors of four children.[2]

2.1.3 The data

Does this generalization, that the only errors in basic word order to occur in the course of English acquisition involve unaccusative verbs, hold up? In (6) through (9) is an exhaustive listing of all postverbal subjects noted in the speech of for children during the specified periods.[3]

(6)   Naomi (1–10–0 to 2–1–3)

unaccusatives   *unergatives*
a. going 'corder   q. sleeping Sandy (2 instances)
b. going it
c. there go horsie (4 instances)
d. slamming door
     Father: that's a door slamming, Nomi
     Nomi: slamming door

e. all gone sun (2 instances)
f. all gone berries
g. byebye sun (2 instances)

    h. is kitty sleep (declarative)
       Naomi: is kitty sleep (no question intonation)
       Mother: is kitty asleep?
    i. is shoes off (declarative)
       Mother: look at the shoes
       Naomi: is shoes off. shoes shoes shoes
       Mother: what about it? yes. those are shoes
    j. is it hard (declarative)
    k. is it fixed (declarative)
    l. is it eat it up (declarative)
    m. is it broke (declarative)
    n. is that Nomi's (declarative)
       Mother: yes, you can have some bread, honey
       Naomi: is that Nomi's. want that [!] dinner
       Mother: want that kind of dinner, too?

    o. there's NP (14 instances) (e.g., there's mommy, there's feet there's
       onesmoke, there's a monkey)

    p. here's NP (8 instances) (e.g., here's it, here's mouth, here's the
       camel)

(7)   Eve (1–6–0 to 1–10–2)

unaccusatives

    a. come car
    b. broke here music

    c. here come Eve
    d. came a man (2 instances)
    e. come Fraser
    f. drop spoon
       Eve: it drop
       Mother: what dropped
       Eve: drop spoon
    g. byebye car (2)
    h. all gone grape juice

    i. there's another one

unergatives

    j. have papa lunch
       Mother: papa's gonna have his
                lunch in there
       Eve: have papa lunch

    k. sneeze Eve
       Mother: she did sneeze, didn't
                she? Lots of sneezes.
       Eve: sneeze Eve (after Eve
                pretends to sneeze)

(8)   Nina (1–11–1 to 2–2–1)

unaccusatives   *unergatives*

a. fall pants   n. drink dolly
b. fall down lady   o. drinking dolly
c. come man, in the box   p. looking duck
                                       Mother: who's looking at the fish
d. all gone the puzzle (3)   Nina: looking duck
e. all gone the coffee   Mother: the ducks are looking at
                                                 the fish
f. is the (giraffe), mine   q. swimming the duck, duck swim-
g. is that your house (declara-   ming
    tive)   r. throw Nina
h. was monkeys climb on that   Mother: what are you doing?
    balloon (declarative)   Nina: throw Nina
                                       Mother: Nina threw the ball?
i. there's NP (15 instances)   s. hop kangaroo (2)
    (e.g., there's the lion,   t. talk mommy kangaroo
    there's a mommy, there's   u. talking baby
    him, there's another)   v. talking baby kangaroo
j. there was monkeys

k. here's NP (25 instances)
    (e.g., here's rabbit, here's
    him, here's my horsie,
    here's a kitty cat)
l. here is my doggie
m. here is big kitty cat in this
    picture

(9)   Peter (1–11–2 to 2–3–0)

unaccusatives   *unergatives*

a. fell down, dump truck   r. push it me
b. broke this (2)
c. come out, bus
d. come Lois
e. go two bolts
f. come a bag
g. broken the light (2)
    Peter: broken the light
    Adult: is the light broken?
h. comes me!

<table>
<tr><td>i.</td><td>here comes choo-choo train</td><td>unergatives</td></tr>
<tr><td>j.</td><td>here comes Jenny again</td><td></td></tr>
</table>

r. pus it me

k. bye-bye wheel (2)

l. all finished this

m. all finished that

n. is that tape (2) (declarative)

o. there's NP (16 instances) (e.g., there's a tape right there, there's the top)

p. here's NP (6 instances) (e.g., here's another one, here's a wheel, here's a daddy)

q. here are they (2 instances)

(10)   Summary of data – Distribution of postverbal subjects according to verb type:

	BE		UNACCUASATIVE	UNERGATIVE
Naomi	28	+	12 (98%)	2 (5%)
Eve	1	+	10 (85%)	2 (15%)
Nina	46	+	7 (84%)	10 (16%)
Peter	26	+	16 (98%)	1 (2%)

There are two points to make about the data presented in (6) through (10). Foremost, in conformity with our predictions for English development and with previous findings, there are very few postverbal subject utterances. For each child, ungrammatical sentences of this kind account for less than 1% of all utterances. Observe that discourse context is provided along with some examples to illustrate the way in which it was determined that a given sentence contained a postverbal subject (as opposed to, i.e. an object), or was intended as a non-interrogative.

Next, note the extent to which postverbal subjects occur with only a small number of verbs. These include not only the more common unaccusative verbs *fall*, *come* and *go*, but also verbs that undergo transitive-unaccusative alternation. The example (6d), which is given in context, shows the child producing verb-subject order immediately after her father produces subject-verb order with the ergative verb *slam*. A similar parent-child discourse pattern in seen in (7f), involving the ergative verb *drop*, and in (9g) with *break*.

Also counted as unaccusatives here are utterances containing *all gone*, *byebye* and *all finished*. Very young children are known for saying things like *all gone juice*. Such productions have traditionally been viewed as primitive routines lacking in internal structure. In contrast, Lebeaux (1988) argues that predicates like *all gone* and *byebye* are unaccusatives (meaning, respectively, *is finished* and *disappeared*). He infers these meanings from contextual descriptions that accompany reports of these utterances in context (in particular, based on Braine, 1963). In Lebeaux's view, the child usually realizes these predicates with postverbal arguments because that is how they are represented in his lexicon. In short, these data provide evidence for Lebeaux's claim that theta assignment, as opposed to Case assignment, determines word order in early speech. While maintaining here that Case plays a large role in the early grammar, I adopt Lebeaux's analysis of utterances like (6e) and (7g).

By far the largest number of postverbal subjects occur with the verb *be*. On the one hand, there are the declaratives with *is* occurring is sentence initial position. The child Naomi (Sachs, 1983) produces most of those (6h-p), although Nina and Peter each produce a couple (i.e. 8f-g, 9n). On the other hand, there are the mostly grammatical cases in which the words *there* and *here* occur in sentence initial position. All but five of these (namely (8j, l, m) and (9q), of which there are two instances) contain the contracted form of the copula, *'s*. In the latter case, it is quite possible that the young child generates *there's* and *here's* as unanalyzed units, rote-learned and used as a discourse formula for the purpose of introducing an object. This has often been proposed as, for example, by Bellugi (1967), Bowerman (1982), Peters (1983).

However, let's explore the consequences of assuming the child's grammar generates sentences like (7i) along the lines of adult grammar. At the very least, this possibility should be considered for utterances which contain be copula in non-contracted form, such as (8m). Following standard analyses of so-called locational constructions with *be* (cf. Burzio, 1986), I assume that *here* and *there* are elements to which no theta role is assigned. They are inserted in [Spec, IP] position at D-structure in constructions with an NP in postverbal position. Although the child is using *there* with a "location" rather than "existential" interpretation, the same analysis holds. In the adult grammar, locative inversion only occurs with ergative verbs (Stowell, 1978). The sentence in (8m), for example, is therefore presumed to appear in its D-structure form. And this implies that the child's grammar represents the [Spec, IP] position.

Returning to the data in (6) through (9), observe that a majority of postverbal subjects in English child language conform to the unaccusative generalization. If a more conservative approach to the data is taken — disregarding the utterances with *there/here* + contracted copula, since they may contain unanalyzed verbal forms — it turns out that over 80% (61 out of 76) of these postverbal subjects distribute with an unaccusative verb or with copular *be*. Of the 15 exceptions to this generalization, the majority were produced by one child, Nina. The remaining three children produced only one or two exceptional postverbal subjects.

Considering only the lexical verbs and disregarding *be*, an average of 75% (45 out of 60) of the lexical verbs occurring with postverbal subjects fall into the unaccusative class. This would not be an interesting observation if in fact the children were using unaccusatives at the same high rate over all utterance types. But a look at the verb frequencies for all four children during this period shows that this is not the case. The percentage of all verb tokens which are unaccusative or undergo transitive-unaccusative alternation ranges from 18 to 26% depending upon the child (mean = 23%). Thus, the proportion of verbs with postverbal subjects that are unaccusative is significantly different from the expected proportion based on overall verb type frequencies (p < .05). This further shows that the child's positioning of the subject is far from random.

In short, the pattern noted at the beginning of this chapter holds up under closer examination. What looked at first glance like counter examples to our prediction that there should be no errors of this sort in

English development turn out not to be. Since the vast majority of the children's word order errors are with verbs that fall into the unaccusative class, these utterances fail to do damage to the claim the acquisition of word order in English is relatively error free. In fact, these errors serve as confirmation for the analysis of unaccusative verbs in English syntax. In short, I claim that the majority of word order errors observed in English acquisition in sentences containing lexical verbs have the structure in (11a or b), where (11a) and (11b) differ only in terms of the location of expletive pro:

(11a)　　Possible S-structures for child utterance (7a)

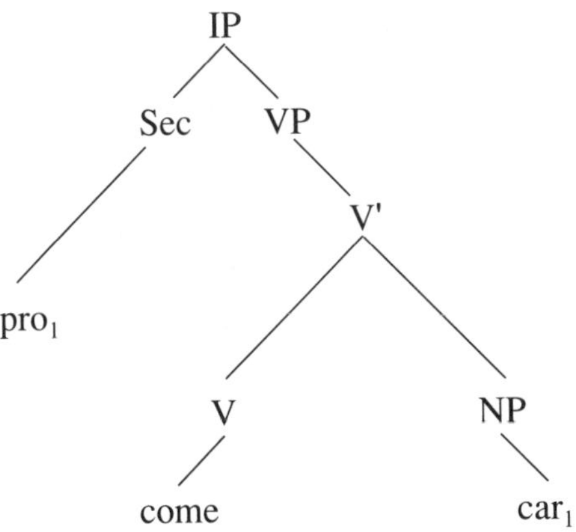

(b)

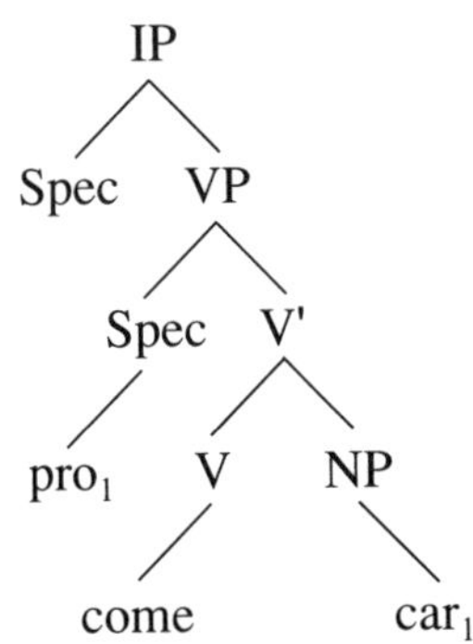

The postverbal subjects found in English child language, then, are not in [Spec, VP] position. The child who says *come car* is simply failing to raise the NP argument out of its base generated position, [NP, VP]. Based on the scarcity of postverbal subjects that do not conform to this generalization in the English data, it can be maintained that the parameter which fixes the order of V' and [Spec, VP] within VP is set very early, in this case to subject-verb order.

These data are readily accounted for by the generalization that the child sometimes fails to raise the NP to [Spec, IP] position. Recall that Case is being assigned to the VP-internal argument by Infl and that what rules out true postverbal subjects is fixed underlying word order and appropriate setting of the parameter which controls inflectional affixation, whereby English lacks main verb raising. This is not to say that the young child always fails to raise the NP, nor is that expected. The idea is that the errors children make are sometimes principled errors, providing a clue to the underlying grammatical representation.[4]

In sum, the examples in (6) through (9) were culled from thousands of verb-containing utterances, and thus represent a very small proportion of the young English speaking child's sentential utterances. What is impressive is the extent to which postverbal subjects recur with only a few verbs across a number of children. The verbs *go, break, come,* and others exemplified above, are members of the class of unaccusative verbs. While it is true that there are exceptions to this generalization (e.g., *throw Nina, hop kangaroo, drink dolly*), the majority of these came from one child, Nina. Furthermore, these cases reflect a clear minority of post-predicate arguments in English child language. There are virtually no "true" postverbal subjects in English child language. This is striking when compared to the facts of French acquisition, to which I now turn.

2.2 POSTVERBAL SUBJECTS IN THE EARLY
GRAMMAR OF FRENCH

2.2.1 Background

Despite a long history of reports in the child language literature concerning the surprising extent of nonstandard word order in early French, this phenomenon has until now not been accorded a grammatical explanation. Previous discussion of these facts centered on potential extragrammatical motivations and analyses. In a 1927 article, Guillaume describes the early stages of sentence formation in French child language. Among the early sentences produced by two children are those shown in (12) and (13):

> (12)   Some postverbal subjects from one 20 month-old male
>   child
>   a. fermée la fenêtre   *closed the window*
>   b. cassées les jambes   *broken the legs*
>   c. morte Marie   *dead Marie*

> (13)   Some postverbal subjects produced by one 14 month-old
>   female child
>   a. fait dodo Foufou   *sleeps Foufou*
>   b. (prom)ener Papa   *walk Papa*
>   c. il a bobo Foufou   *he's hurt Foufou*

These postverbal subject utterances occur side-by-side with utterances in which the subject appears in preverbal position or is missing altogether. Guillaume notes this variability in word order, but argues that it is superficial:

One should not be deceived by some inversions. If (the child) says 'Fermée la fenêtre' (= shut the window), it is because he is imitating 'elle est fermée, la fenêtre' (= It is shut, the window).[5]

Other developmentalists studying French acquisition, both before and after Guillaume, report extensive variability in word order (Bloch,

1924; Sinclair, 1973; Sabeau-Jouannet, 1975; Lightbown, 1977; Clark, 1985). But the explanation given for this variability has remained largely unchanged since Guillaume's time. The idea is that a child outputting utterances like those in (12) and (13a, b) is simultaneously dropping the true subject and producing a right-dislocated (extrasentential) constituent. (13c) is an example of successful production of a right dislocation, one in which the subject pronoun is not omitted. Clark (1985) emphasizes the role of adult right dislocation structures in leading children to use postverbal subjects, noting that evidence regarding the intonation pattern of such constructions is crucial to determining whether they are truly word order errors, or pragmatically governed variations as in adult speech, or merely sequences of single words.

This approach makes undeniable sense. There is obviously some truth in the claim that the extent of word order variability in the child's language must reflect, to some degree, that in the adult language. Because subject pronouns are unstressed and dislocated NP's are presumably salient, the child might simply perceive an adult utterance such as "il va dormir le chien" (*he goes to sleep the dog*) as "va dormir le chien" (*goes to sleep the dog*). Experimental work has indeed shown that infants and young children are sensitive to intonational properties of the input (Reid and Schreiber, 1982; Pye, 1983; Gleitman *et al.*, 1988). The issue I wish to address here is the nature of the child grammar which produces the sentences in (12) and (13). How are these sentences syntactically represented? Is there any evidence that the grammar which produces them differs from the adult grammar? I turn now to a careful examination of subject distribution in four French children in an attempt to answer these questions.

2.2.2 *The data*

In contrast to the case of English child language, where ungrammatical postverbal subjects account for less than 1% of the overall data, there are a startling number of postverbal subjects in the output

of the four French children studied. Examples from each child are
shown in (14) through (17):

(14)   *Nathalie*[6]

a. manger la poupée (1–9–3)
   (*eat the doll*)

b. tomber papa (2–0–1)
   (*fall papa*)

c. assis la poupée (2–0–1)
   (*seated the doll*)

d. est a poupée le couteau
   (2–2–2)
   (*is the doll's the knife*)

e. pas dormir bébé (2–2–2)
   (*not sleep baby*)

f. dormir bébé (2–0–1)
   (*sleep baby*)

(15)   *Philippe*

a. est chaud camion (2–2–0)
   (*is hot truck*)

b. dormir là Michel (2–2–1)
   (*sleep there Michel*)

c. travailler moi (2–2–1)
   (*work me*)

d. est froid le camion (2–2–0)
   (*is cold the truck*)

e. veux tourner moi (2–2–1)
   (*want to turn me*)

f. écrit Madeleine (2–2–2)
   (*writes Madeleine*)

(16)   *Daniel*

a. bois peu moi (1–8–1)
   (*drink little me*)

b. pleure clown (1–8–3)
   (*cries clown*)

c. tout mangé Patsy (1–8–3)
   (*ate all Patsy*)

d. plait pas monsieur (1–9–3)
   (*don't like the male doll*)

e. est tombé papachou
   (1–10–2)
   (*fell the papa doll*)

f. dormir petit bébé (1–11–1)
   (*sleep little baby*)

(17)   *Grégoire*

    a. est dans la boîte l'avion
       (2–3–0)
       (*is in the box the plane*)

    b. veut monter Grégoire
       (1–10–0)
       (*want to climb Grégoire*)

    c. tombe Victor (2–0–1)
       (*falls Victor*)

    d. va à fac papa (2–0–1)
       (*goes to work papa*)

    e. fait une maison Victor
       (2–3–0)
       (*makes a house Victor*)

    f. a chanté Victor (2–1–3)
       (*sang Victor*)

In fact, postverbal lexical subjects outnumber preverbal lexical subjects for an extended period in all four children. In (18) are the percentages of lexical subjects that occur postverbally for each child at
each transcript stage examined:

(18)   Proportion of lexical subjects that occur postverbally (not
       including right dislocations with coreferent subject clitics)

    Grégoire

    G1 (1–9–2)   68% (11/16)
    G2 (1–10–0)   84% (48/57)
    G3 (1–10–3)   89% (23/26)
    G4 (1–11–3)   83% (20/24)
    G5 (2–0–1)   74% (17/23)
    G6 (2–1–3)   55% (5/9)
    G7 (2–3–0)   69% (13/19)

    Nathalie

    N1 (1–9–3)   72% (31/43)
    N2 (1–10–1)   88% (41/51)
    N4 (2–0–1)   89% (24/27)
    N6 (2–2–2)   12% (6/50)
    N7 (2–3–2)   5% (1/20)

    Daniel

    D1 (1–8–1)   71% (10/14)
    D2 (1–8–3)   67% (14/21)

D3 (1–9–3)   29% (4/14)
D4 (1–10–2)   31% (16/51)
D5 (1–11–1)   70% (19/27)

Philippe

P1 (2–1–3)   50% (7/14)
P2 (2–2–0)   82% (18/22)
P3 (2–2–1)   74% (28/38)
P4 (2–2–2)   84% (26/31)
P7 (2–3–0)   74% (14/19)

The reader can observe that the overall number of lexical subjects (in pre- or postverbal positions) is not very high, when one considers that the sentences counted above were culled from thousands of utterances. But there is clear consistency across and within children at an early period in the preferential placement of lexical subjects to the right of the verb. From the perspective of current syntactic theory, this robust finding arguably reflects the base-generated position of the subject. The model's predictions for word order in the development of French are indeed fulfilled.

In order to determine how the postverbal subject construction is arrived at, it is useful to consider the relationship of subject placement to tense and transitivity. Postverbal subjects occur in both finite and nonfinite clauses, with both transitive and intransitive verbs. Examples of postverbal subjects in various sentence types are shown in (19):

(19)   Additional postverbal subjects

    [+ finite, + transitive]

    VOS: a. a bobo fesse Nathalie (Nathalie, 2–0–1)
                 (*has a booboo Nathalie*)
    VOS: b. fait du bruit la voiture (Philippe, 2–2–1)
                 (*makes noise the car*)
    VSO: c. pousses toi sandales (Daniel, 1–8–3)
                 (*push you sandals*)
    VSO: d. veut encore Adrien du pain (Grégoire, 2–1–3)
                 (*wants more Adrien$_{subs}$ bread*)

[+ finite, − transitive]

unaccusative: e. monte la main (Grégoire, 1–10–3)
              (*climbs the hand*)
unaccusative: f. est tombé Dani (Daniel, 1–8–3)
              (*fell Dani*)
unergative: g. travaille papa (Philippe, 2–2–1)
              (*works daddy*)
unergative: h. pleure bébé (Nathalie, 1–11–2)
              (*cries baby*)

[− finite, +transitive]

VOS: i. faire boum sur le camion maman (Philippe, 2–1–3)
         (*make boom on the truck mommy*)
VOS: j. manger salade Adrien (Grégoire, 1–9–2)
         (*eat sald Adrien*)
VSO: k. couper couteau bol (Daniel, 1–8–3)
         (*cut knife$_{subs}$ bowl*)
VSO: l. acheter moi bébé (Daniel (1–8–3)
         (*buy me$_{subs}$ baby*)

[− finite, −transitive]

unaccusative: m. monter Grégoire (Grégoirc, 1–10–0)
              (*climb Grégoire*)
unaccusative: n. sorti les vaches (Philippe, 2–2–3)
              (*left the cows*)
unergative: o. encore manger la poupée (Nathalie, 1–9–3)
              (*again eat the doll*)
unergative: p. dessiner le crayon (Grégoire, 2–0–1)
              (*draw the crayon*)

As opposed to English acquisition, where we found postverbal subjects exclusively in the context of unaccusative verbs, French children
produce postverbal subjects with both transitive verbs and unergative
intransitive verbs. Looking first at the transitive cases, both VOS and
VSO orders are found, although VOS and V-Complement-S construc-

tions are by far more common. The existence of both orders suggests that there are multiple ways to arrive at a postverbal subject. While the VSO form is readily derived via underlying S-V' order in conjunction with the verb raising to Infl, the VOS form requires underlying V'-S order or right dislocation for its derivation. I will return to the issue of postverbal subjects in transitive constructions shortly.

Looking now at the intransitive cases, both unaccusatives and unergatives are found. As in English, the post-predicate argument in the French unaccusatives in (19) is analyzed as a D-structure object. In the unergative examples, the argument following the verb is clearly an agent. For these cases, then, I assume the analysis in (20):

(20)   S-structure for child utterance (19h)

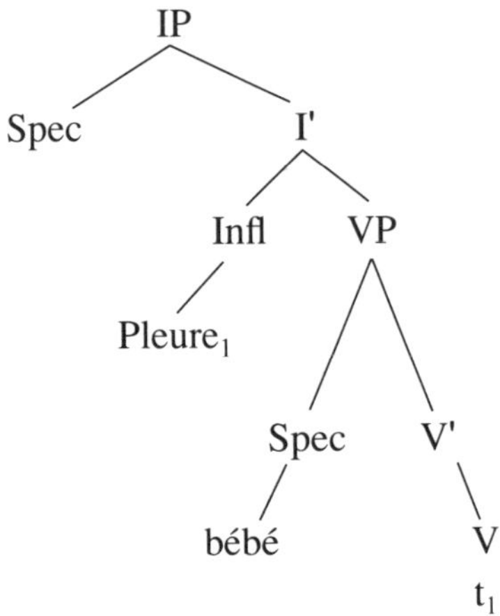

According to this analysis, the postverbal position of the subject is derived as a result of the VP-internal generation of the subject and the leftward movement of the verb to Infl. As described in the previous chapter, the NP subject *bébé* receives nominative Case through Infl government.

While this analysis holds for intransitive unergative utterances, what about transitive utterances? Finite VSO constructions, of which a few examples were observed, conform to the same derivation. On the assumption of underlying S-V-O order and V-to-I, V-S-O word order ensues. Further evidence that children derive and represent VSO order comes from a well known comprehension study. Sinclair & Bronkart (1972) report that a verb-noun-noun sequence in which the arguments are semantically symmetric (e.g. *push-boy-girl*) is interpreted by 82% of French three-to-four years olds as action-agent-patient (rather than action-patient-agent). In other words, there is a strong preference to interpret the first NP as subject, in the absence of any semantic cue to the contrary. This is expected if the child's grammar indeed derives VSO order from VP-internal subjects in conjunction with verb raising.

VOS constructions, however, are more problematic for this analysis. A subject generated in [Spec, VP] position will not end up, as a result of verb raising alone, in sentence final position of a transitive at S-structure. VOS, V-complement-S and postverbal subjects in complex tenses are nonetheless fairly common in French child language. Assuming there is no V'-raising, there are two potential derivations for them. One possibility is right dislocation of the subject (assumed to be adjunction to IP or VP), which is, in any event, quite characteristic of adult spoken French.[7] Rightward movement of the subject to an adjoined position results in sentence final placement of the subject no matter how complex the verbal tense or what complements the verb takes.

The other possibility is base generation of [Spec,VP] to the right of V'. Although it goes against the intuition that the direction of theta role assignment in French parallels that in English, this analysis readily accounts for much of the child language data. In particular, the large number of infinitivals with postverbal subjects found (see, for example, (16f), (19j)) would seem to suggest base V'-S order. Yet the analysis of such utterances is far from clear. French infinitives with the -*er* infinitival ending are homophonous with past participles, as well as with the regular second person plural/polite form. Therefore, an utterance such as (19j), with an apparent infinitive, may well contain a past participle, while missing subject and auxiliary. Lightbown (1977) notes this ambiguity but argues that, since young children's talk tends to concern the here and now, the past participle interpretation of these verbal forms is questionable. On the basis of this reasoning, she transcribes all verbs with this ending that occur in the absence of an auxiliary as infinitives. In my view, the past participle interpretation is not ruled out in this fashion. The past participle occurs both with and without an auxiliary in the French acquisition data. It is sometimes used as an adjective, in which case it is describing the present. And it is sometimes used as a verbal participle, in which case it can describe the immediate past. Since children's talk is obviously not constrained to refer to the present moment only, the latter interpretation of the nonfinite form is arguably available. Since a verb in nonfinite form may well be a past participle, sentences of the form in (19j) do not necessarily reflect the base word order. This is because past participles may undergo short movement to Infl, to a position below that of negation (specifically, Agr-O) (Pollock, 1988). In fact, this analysis is necessary to account for nonfinite VSO cases such as (19k) and (19l). Since the ambiguity in interpretation of nonfinite verbal forms is impossible to resolve in all cases, the existence of utterances with postverbal subjects and nonfinite verbs can not be relied on to determine the underlying structure of the sentence in French child language.

There are, however, additional motivations for assuming that [Spec, VP] is generated to the right of V' in French child language. Recall Sportiche's (1988; Koopman and Sportiche, 1988) claim that French lacks fixed ordering of major constituents under VP, since French, but not English, regularly exhibits inverted word in certain contexts. As a further consideration, Rosen (1989) argues that the V'-S possibility readily accounts for causitive formation in French and other Romance languages.[8] Right-branching VP-internal subjects have also, for various reasons concerning various languages, been postulated by, among others, Kitagawa (1986), Borer (1986a), Contreras (1987), and Bonet (1989). One argument against the claim that French child grammar includes optional ordering of the major constituents under VP is that it does away with a unified approach to underlying word order in French and English acquisition. It implies that the parameter controlling this aspect of word order is set early and differently in the two languages, in the English case to fixed S-V' order and in the French case to optional ordering.

In my view, there is not yet enough evidence to decide between the right dislocation explanation and the optional V-S' explanation for VOS utterances. A sentence like (19j), therefore, has the form either in (21a) or in (21b):[9]

(21a)   S-structure for utterance (19j)

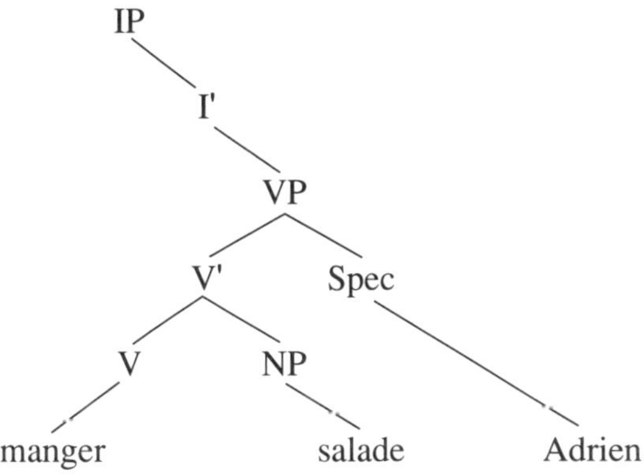

(b)

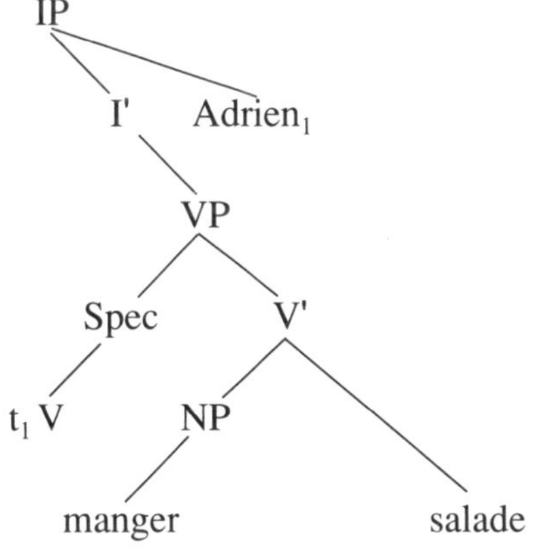

Under either analysis, we are forced to abandon the generalization that word order in English and French child language is differentiated only by the role of verb raising in the latter. French child language demonstrates much more variability in subject placement than verb raising alone can explain. A further indication that one of these two mechanisms is necessary to account for the observed variability in word order comes from the absence of anything approaching a significant correlation between verb raising and postverbal subjects.

Given Sinclair and Bronkart's (1972) finding, described above, and the fact that a small number of VSO constructions are found in the French child data, I assume that verb raising plays a role in the derivation of postverbal subjects. However, if all postverbal subjects were the result of verb raising, then it follows that only raised verbs should occur with postverbal subjects. This is clearly not the case. Nor is it found that, for all children, explicitly tensed verbs occur with a higher proportion of postverbal lexical subjects than nonfinite verbs (i.e. infinitives or participles). This is shown in (22):

(22)   Proportion of lexical subjects in postverbal position, according to verb type (includes utterances with coreferent subject clitics)

	[+Finite]			[−Finite]
Grégoire	87% (N=116)	>	73% (N=52)
Nathalie	34% (N=23)	<	73% (N=103)
Daniel	74% (N=35)	<	76% (N=22)
Philippe	84% (N=119)	>	76% (N=26)

With the exception of the child Nathalie, postverbal subjects in finite clauses do outnumber postverbal subjects in nonfinite clauses. But only two of the children, Grégoire and Philippe, produce a higher proportion of post-predicate lexical subjects in the context of explicitly tensed verbs. For Daniel, the proportions are roughly equal. For Nathalie, on the other hand, postverbal subjects in finite clauses are much less frequent than for other children. The proportion of postverbal subjects in nonfinite clauses is similar across all four children.

Nor is a definitive verb raising/postverbal subject correlation any

more in evidence when we examine these proportions over the course
of development. This is illustrated in (23) – (26):

(23)   Proportion of postverbal subjects according to verb type
        and age: Philippe

	[+Finite]		[−Finite]
2–1–3	86% (N=19)	>	33% (N=2)
2–2–0	87% (N=26)	<	100% (N=7)
2–2–1	80% (N=37)	>	67% (N=2)
2–2–2	89% (N=24)	>	82% (N=9)
2–3–0	76% (N=13)	<	86% (N=6)

(24)   Proportion of postverbal subjects according to verb type
        and age: Nathalie

	[+Finite]		[−Finite]
1–9–3	0% (0/0)	<	72% (N=31)
1–10–2	75% (N=6)	<	92% (N=45)
2–0–1	100% (N=4)	>	88% (N=22)
2–2–2	17% (N=5)	<	21% (N=5)
2–3–2	31% (N=8)	>	0% (0/1)

(25)   Proportion of postverbal subjects according to verb type
        and age Grégoire

	[+Finite]		[−Finite]
1–9–2	100% (N=10)	>	17% (N=1)
1–10–0	89% (N=25)	>	82% (N=28)
1–10–3	100% (N=19)	>	70% (N=7)
1–11–3	91% (N=21)	>	75% (N=6)
2–0–1	86% (N=18)	>	70% (N=7)
2–1–3	60% (N=6)	<	100% (N=1)
2–3–0	74% (N=17)	<	100% (N=2)

(26)   Proportion of postverbal subjects according to verb type
        and age: Daniel

	[+Finite]		[−Finite]
1–8–1	75% (N=3)	>	70% (N=7)
1–8–3	58% (N=7)	<	82% (N=9)
1–9–3	33% (N=1)	>	27% (N=3)
1–10–2	39% (N=11)	>	22% (N=5)
1–11–1	81% (N=25)	>	75% (N=6)

Glancing over these tables, note that the percentage of finite clauses with postverbal subjects as opposed to preverbal subjects remains high throughout, with the exception of Nathalie during the 2–2–2 to 2–3–2 period. Of the four children studied, Nathalie is the only one to manifest widespread subject raising at any period. In fact, in Nathalie's case, the acquisition of subject raising (as evidenced by preverbal subjects in finite clauses) coincides with the acquisition of verb raising (as evidenced by the disappearance of nonfinite verbs). This pattern is not typical of the other children. Three out of the four children produce few raised subjects (i.e. preverbal subjects in tensed clauses) at any point studied. Nathalie is also exceptional in that she manifests an early period (1–9–3 to 2–0–1) in which finite verbs are extremely rare. If such a pattern is found in future studies of very young French speaking children, then this would be strong evidence for a pre-verb raising phases in the acquisition of French syntax. As it stands, the evidence is only suggestive in this regard. Returning to the main concern here, the majority of lexical subjects in Nathalie's many nonfinite utterances appear in postverbal position.

Looking at (23) and (25), the initial transcripts of both Philippe and Grégoire contain a majority of preverbal subjects in nonfinite clauses, alongside the clear minority of preverbal lexical subjects in finite clauses. This is exactly the pattern predicted if verb raising is largely responsible for the sentence-final position. Given that this pattern characterizes two of the many language samples, it constitutes suggestive support for the verb raising account of postverbal subjects.[10]

In short, there appear to be multiple ways to derive sentence-final subjects in French child language, as in the adult language. I have considered four possibilities in this chapter. The first was raising of inflected verbs. Main verbs raise in French, but not in English; French children produce true postverbal subjects, but English children do not. Verb raising therefore provides an elegant explanation for a difference between French and English acquisition. However, movement of tensed verbs fails to account for all the French word order data, and in particular for the cases V-S order in nonfinite clauses. It was suggested that short movement of the participle to a low position within Infl can account for nonfinite VS and VSO. Verb raising alone, however, cannot account for cases of VOS order. Two accounts for VOS order are available. One is rightward adjunction of the subject and the other is optional V'-S order at D-structure. Just as this ambiguity remains in current descriptions of adult French syntax, the developmental data is insufficient to decide between these two competing hypotheses.

Briefly, let's consider the analysis of preverbal subjects. Because the children at the stage I am describing generally fail to generate subjects either to the left of a negative (as I will show in chapter 3) or to the left of a tensed verb, the only likely representation for a preverbal subject construction such as *Moi dessiner le mer* (Me draw$_{-fin}$ the sea), produced by Daniel 1–10–2, is as in (27), details aside:

(27)

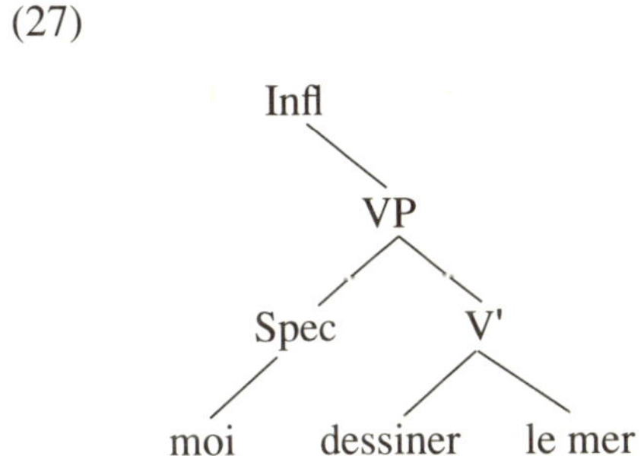

Preverbal subjects with nonfinite verbs, on this approach, are underived structures for the child. In these cases, both the subject and the verb, being nonfinite, appear to have failed to raise. Presumably, intransitive sentences with postverbal subjects and inflected verbs reflect the raising of the verb to Infl while the subject stays in place within the VP. Sentences with preverbal lexical subjects and inflected verbs would of course entail movement of the subject: if the verb raises to Infl, then the only way to recover S-V order is if the subject moves leftward as well, which does not seem to be happening. Specifically, less than 5% of the early data necessitate a subject raising analysis. We can remain undecided between an analysis in which postverbal subjects result from verb raising and one in which they result from lack of fixed ordering under VP and still maintain that the subject is generated VP-internally. In addition, under both analyses, we can account for over 95% of the data encountered in terms of a developmental delay in subject raising. The VP-internal subject hypothesis and the additional observation that subject NPs generally fail to raise at an early stage in French child language can account for most of the spontaneous word order data. While the data may not decide between the various hypotheses concerning underlying order of the verbal projection and it's specifier, there is decisive evidence that Guillaume was wrong to attend only to the superficial similarity between children's postverbal subjects and right dislocations in the spoken adult language.

The reader will note that I have so far omitted discussion of prononimal and null subjects, as well as discussion of lexical subject raising. Each of these issues will be addressed in later chapters. It has been the main concern of this chapter to show that French child language has true postverbal subjects, and to argue that these are unraised VP-internal subjects. In order to substantiate further the verb raising derivation of some of these utterances, I turn in the next two chapters to the evidence that French child grammar represents a distinction between finite and nonfinite clauses. The data on negation, analyzed in Chapter 3, that on verbal inflection in Chapter 4, and that on subject clitics in Chapter 5 leave no doubt as to the French two-year old's knowledge of Infl.

2.2.3 *A glance at word order in Italian child languages*

It is interesting to note that the overall distribution of utterances in early French language is quite similar to patterns which emerge in the study of Italian child language. Bates (1976) presents figures, based on two children, which describe the extent of the various permutations of subject-verb-object word order in Italian child language.[11] (28) contains a retabulation of her data:

(28)

Claudia, from 1– 3–3 (MLU 1.85) to 1–9–3 (MLU 3.66)
Total number of postverbal subjects = 88 (73% of all overt subjects)

verb-subject: 76
object-verb-subject: 6
verb-subject-object: 5
verb-object-subject: 1

Francesco, from 1–4–0 (MLU 1.65) to 2–0–2 (MLU 2.25)
Total number of postverbal subjects = 82 (77% of all overt subjects)

verb-subject: 61
object-verb-subject: 8
verb-subject-object: 4
verb-object-subject: 9

For the child Claudia, 73% of overt subjects appear in postverbal position. For Francesco, 77% of overt subjects appear in postverbal position.[12] These figures are generally comparable to the findings for subject distribution in French child language, further suggesting that French child language generates postverbal subjects in a manner comparable to a so-called free inversion language like Italian.

2.3 CASE ASSIGNMENT

Recently, it has been proposed that child language is characterized by the absence of inflection at early stages (Guilfoyle and Noonan, 1988; Kazman, 1988; Aldridge, 1988). In Guilfoyle and Noonan's model, functional structure matures sometime after the second birthday. Before that time, children are said to represent only lexical categories. They are presumably unable to inflect verbs or assign nominative Case to the subject.[13] One insurmountable problem for the theory that inflection is simply absent from two year-old grammar is the fact that complex inflectional paradigms are acquired very early by the child learning, for example, Polish (Weist *et al*, 1984) or Italian (Bates, 1976; Hyams, 1984).

One outcome of adopting the VP-internal subject analysis is that it can capture the same descriptive generalization as the no-Infl approach without assuming that the child's grammar is inflectionless. That is, inflection is not integrated into the clause until the child acquires a mechanism for attaching inflectional affixes. At the same time, we can assume that the Case filter, a principle of universal grammar, is operational. According to Koopman and Sportiche (1988), the underlying VP-internal subject structure conforms to a prerequisite configuration for nominative Case assignment in languages in which subject raising is not obligatory. In the Koopman-Sportiche framework and elsewhere, inflection head-governs the maximal projection of the verb and it specifier. Tensed inflection can thereby assign Case to the VP-internal subject (cf. also Bonet, 1989).

I briefly consider another possibility for the assignment of Case to the VP-internal subject in early grammar. Assuming that the Case filter holds and that Infl does not assign Case to the underived subject, the only potential Case assigners are the verb itself or a projection of the verb. Li (1985) argues that all verbs, including intransitives, assign Case and that postverbal subjects in Chinese can be assigned accusative Case by the verb, nominative Case failing to be assigned into the VP. Or, adopting the notion of inherent or D-structure Case, in which Case assignment is in direct association with theta role assignment, V-bar might assign Case to the VP-internal subject position. One consideration which works against this general approach is that Case assignment that overlaps with theta role assignment is vacuous as a licensing condition. Second, inherent Cases, such as the genitive and oblique Cases, have generally been said to conform to constraints of directionality (cf. Chomsky, 1981; 1986a), which would not hold for Case assigned by V' to [Spec, VP], given optional ordering. Finally, this approach raises the question of what would cause the child to abandon inherent assignment of Case to the VP-internal subject.

I maintain instead that Infl is "present" and can assign nominative Case structurally to the VP-internal subject in early grammar, whether the subject is generated to the left or to the right of the verb. Furthermore, I suggest that the optionality of tensed inflection in early child language does not indicate a lack of abstract tense. Rather, the base generation of verbs in infinitival or participial form, combined with the occasional omission of the auxiliary verb along with the subject, leads the child to output apparently nonfinite clauses. Thus, I am assuming that the VP-internal subject configuration meets the structural requirements for the assignment of nominative Case in the context of a nonfinite clause, along the lines of the Aux-to-Comp rule of Italian (Rizzi, 1982) and extensions of that mechanism (e.g. Borer, 1989; Huang, 1989). According to Huang (1989), in providing a government-based account of null subjects and nominative Case assignment in Chinese, the finiteness of a clause may be determined in terms of the potential occurrence of overt Aux (i.e. tensed Infl). In clauses which are potentially finite but which contain a zero-morpheme in Aux, Aux still governs and assigns nominative Case to the lexical subject, or licenses *pro* in subject position. In short, I am proposing that the occurrence of lexical subjects with infinitives in French child language may be viewed as evidence that these clauses are not marked as nonfinite on an abstract level.

There are two major consequences of this analysis of Case assignment. First, null subjects in French child language are accounted for naturally, as VP-internal subjects. According to Rizzi (1986a), the crucial licensing relation on *pro* is Case assignment by a designated head, where membership in the set of licensing heads defines a crosslinguistic parameter. I am also assuming, therefore, that Infl constitutes a Case assigning head in French child language, just as Koopman and Sportiche (1988) argue for the class of languages which license null subjects. Given the VP-internal subject D-structure, and the definition of government adopted by Koopman and Sportiche, whereby Infl governs the VP and its specifier, then infl in this configuration assigns Case to the VP-internal subject position. Thus, a *pro* subject is licensed in exactly the same configuration that a lexical subject is assigned structural Case, namely under directional government (Adams, 1987).

What is the motivation for taking Infl to be a Case assigning head in child language? Recall that, in the Koopman-Sportiche framework, the parameter which determines whether or not the VP-internal subject must raise at S-structure merely specifies whether or not Infl is an obligatory raising category. In English and French, it is argued, Infl is an obligatory raising category; in Italian, it is not. A language in which Infl is not a raising category is by definition a language in which Infl assigns structural nominative Case. On the basis of this insight, it may be argued that since Infl is not an obligatory raising category in early French language, Infl serves to assign Case into the VP. If Infl is a Case assigning head in French child language, what forces subject raising, and the loss of null subjects, over the course of development? Though my central claims here do not depend on this point, I suggest that the governing status of Infl need not change. This leads to what I see as the second major consequence of this analysis of nominative Case assignment in child language. As I will discuss more fully in chapter 7, it is possible that structural assignment of nominative Case is retained in both languages. It most certainly is in French, and may well be in English, according to Contreras' (1987) analysis of simple affirmative sentences in English.

2.4 SUMMARY

In this chapter, it was argued, contrary to Kitagawa (1986), that the VP-internal subject in English is a left-branching sister of the V', one of the options defined by the VP-internal subject parameter. The data presented here indicate that the English-speaking child knows at a very early age that subjects are generated to the left of the verb in the target language. The few exceptions to standard subject-verb order observed in the natural production data turn out to involve unaccusative verbs. The near absence of word order errors in English child language is striking in contrast to the word order variability found in French child language. While some of the verbs occurring with postverbal subjects in French child language are unaccusatives, many are not.

The postverbal subject data from the four French speaking children provide what is perhaps the strongest evidence that the subject is generated within the VP. I considered the possibility that the position of the subject within the VP is not fixed in French. Sportiche (1988) claims that this is the correct description of French, based on the fact that French exhibits overt postverbal subjects in cases of licensed inversion in certain interrogative structures. The important point, however, was the underived status of some postverbal subjects in French child language, a point which follows whether or not V'-[Spec, VP] order is fixed. As mentioned above, many, including Borer (1986a), Contreras (1987) and Bonet (1989), have argued that postverbal subjects in Romance languages are base generated in postverbal position within the VP, as opposed to being adjoined to the VP.

NOTES

[1] This is not to say that unaccusatives with preverbal subjects are absent during this period. Rather, the claim is that the derivation of unaccusative sentences leads to the expectation of word order errors of the observed type during acquisition, whether on an error-type basis only or as the result of the immature English grammar systematically assigning nominative Case to VP-internal positions.

[2] See Pierce (1989) for a review of data from additional children.

[3] This excludes utterances with demonstrative pronouns followed by be, which will be discussed later on.

[4] The question arises how the extent and character of subject postposing in child language relates to the child's linguistic input. Not surprisingly, a search through the maternal speech data revealed only a few instances of subject postposing in non-interrogatives, with the exception of existential and locative inversion with *be*. The other exceptional cases involved the mother either imitating something ungrammatical that the child had just said or repeating the child's name at the end of an utterance in the form of an apostrophe (not to be confused with right dislocation). In terms of unaccusative verbs, the input contains clear evidence of transitive-

unaccusative alternation in the case of verbs like *break* and *close*. Again, locative inversion with *come* and *go* provides evidence to the child that those verbs are unaccusative. The child's use of *fall*, and a few other creative cases discussed above, appear to reflect either the child's over-generalization of the transitive-unaccusative rule, or an occasional absence of NP-raising.

5 Guillaume, 1927 (English translation by E. Clark in Ferguson and Slobin (eds.), 1973).

6 It should be noted that the child Nathalie uses some novel words as verbs, especially during an early period. For example, she says "myamyam" as opposed to "manger" to mean either *food* or *eat*. My interpretation of these forms follows Lightbown (1977), who based her interpretation on discourse context and on translations offered by Nathalie's mother.

7 Right dislocation in the spoken adult language, however, always involves a coindexed clitic. The only exception to this is heavy NP shift, described as basically free adjunction of the subject to IP (Deprez, 1988).

8 In addition, it is interesting to note that there is relatively little evidence of object dislocation in the early child data, although object and subject dislocation are common in adult spoken French.

9 For simplicity, I have assumed in (21) that the verbs is an infinitive and does not raise. In any event, movement of verb here is string vacuous.

10 In order to perform a more controlled test of the verb raising account of postverbal subjects, I repeated the measurements in (23) through (26) on a subset of the class of children's verbs. Specifically, I considered only intransitive unergative verbs, as these are the most likely candidates for a verb raising derivation of the postverbal subject. The search included the regular verbs *manger* (*to eat*), *pleurer* (*to cry*), *dormir* (*to sleep*), *travailler* (*to work*), *tousser* (*to cough*), *dessiner* (*to draw*), *chanter* (*to sing*). The results mirrored the pattern described in the text.

11 Bates excludes copular constructions and wh-questions from these tabulations.

12 In these data, the category *subject* encompasses both pronouns and other noun phrases. Notes, however, that subject pronouns in Italian are so-called strong form pronominals, not clitics. Thus, the inclusion of subject pronouns in the Italian data on subjects and word order does not impede comparison to French usage of NP subjects.

13 Bloom (1988) and Lebeaux (1988) also present arguments to the effect that the Case filter is not operational in the early grammar.

CHAPTER 3

NEGATION

This chapter examines the structure of negation in early English and French child language.[1] Given the assumption of underlying VP-internal subjects and the possibility that the early grammar does not force subject raising, one prediction of the model is that negative sentences with unraised VP-internal subjects will surface in English and French child language. Indeed, negation provides a test case for the model because the issue of whether the subject is situated in [Spec, IP] or [Spec, VP] is resolved by its location relative to the negative element. Following Pollock (1989) and Zanutinni (1989), among others, I assume that the negative element is either a VP-adjunct or in [Spec, NegP] and that its position to the left of the verb is fixed.

As you will see below, the prediction of transparently internal subjects in negatives is confirmed, corroborating Bellugi's (1967) description of just such a stage in the acquisition of English negation. Perhaps more surprising are the results of comparing French and English in this domain. While subject initial negatives are dispreferred in both populations at the start, only in English development does this situation clearly change. That is, S-structure VP-internal subjects quickly disappear in English but remain in French. This suggests that the optional subject raising feature of French reflects a default parameter setting. The discussion in this chapter will also touch upon the verb-movement parameter. In particular, the data suggest that the parameter distinguishing modes of inflectional affixation in the two languages is already set by the time of the earliest examined transcripts, before two years of age. This particular observation is examined further in the next chapter.

3.1 NEGATION IN ENGLISH CHILD LANGUAGE

3.1.1 Background

The data discussed in this section conform to results originally presented by Bellugi (Brown and Bellugi, 1964; Klima and Bellugi, 1966; Bellugi, 1967). Bellugi described an initial stage in the development of negative structures as including negative-initial utterances like the following:

(1)   Some of Bellugi's Stage 1 examples (Brown and Bellugi, 1964; Klima and Bellugi, 1966)

        a. no play that
        b. no tear book
        c. no the sun shining
        d. no I see truck

There has since been some debate concerning the status of utterances like those in (1). Some have argued that sentences of this forms are only produced by children with the intention of saying, for example, "No, in fact I did see the truck" or "No, in fact I want to tear the book" (Bloom, 1970). As such, they would be instances of anaphoric negation, in which the negative negates a prior sentence in the discourse, while the sentence immediately following the negative is actually affirmative.

Others have maintained that children produce negative initial utterances to varying degrees with both anaphoric and nonanaphoric meaning (DeVilliers and DeVilliers, 1985). It is the nonanaphoric type, being a true negative, that is of interest here. Of course, only contextual information can determine the intended meaning of an individual sentence of this form. (2) contains examples of the sort of context that can be used to identify the nonanaphoric cases[2]:

(2)   Context of utterance (1b)

        Mother: Won't you tear it up?

Child: **No, no tear book.**
Mother: No, you won't tear the book up?

Context of utterance (ld)

Mother: Did you see the truck?
Child: **No I see truck.**
Mother: No, you didn't see it. There goes one.

3.1.2 The data

Once again, the spontaneous speech of four children is considered, this time in order to evaluate Bellugi's characterization of negation in child English and the prediction that the early grammar generates structures like those in (1). The tables in (3) break the distribution of overt subject negatives down according to age and whether the subject occurs to the left or the right of the verb (i.e in [Spec, IP] or [Spec, VP] position) for each individual child.[3]

(3)

Eve's negatives

	unraised subject ([Spec, VP])	raised subject ([Spec, IP])
AGE		
1–8–0 to 1–9–2	9 (90%)	1
1–11–0 to 2–0–2	1	35 (97%)

Naomi's negatives

	unraised subject ([Spec, VP])	raised subject ([Spec, IP])
AGE		
1–9–1 to 1–10–0	0	0
2–0–1 to 2–1–3	0	10 (100%)

Peter's negatives

	unraised subject ([Spec, VP])	raised subject ([Spec, IP])
AGE		
2–0–1 to 2–1–0	0	0
2–3–0 to 2–3–3	0	10　(100%)

Nina's negatives

	unraised subject ([Spec, VP])	raised subject ([Spec, Ip])
AGE		
1–11–2 to 2–1–0	6　(100%)	0
2–1–3 to 2–2–1	2	26　(93%)

Two distinct patterns are observed. Two of the children, Naomi and Peter, produce no overt unraised subjects in negatives. Although overt subjects are placed to the left of the negative as soon as they begin to appear, overt subjects in negatives are completely absent from the youngest transcripts of both of these children. The remaining children, Eve and Nina, display an intriguing developmental shift. They produce a majority of overt subjects in sentence medial or internal position during the youngest speech samples, but within a matter of weeks the relevant proportions reverse. For Eve, while 90% of her overt subjects are VP-internal during the first period considered, only 3% (one instance) are during the second period considered. For Nina, while 100% of her overt subjects are VP-internal during the first period, only 7% are during the second. This developmental shift cannot be explained by changes in general linguistic-cognitive measures of growth, such as M.L.U. or overall processing capacity, since an equivalent number of uttered words occurs in negatives of the form Neg-Subject-V and in negatives of the form Subject-Neg-V. However, a change in the grammar itself, such as setting a parameter at a value which excludes overt subjects to the right of a negative element, readily accounts for the observed trend.

There are admittedly few overt subject negatives produced during the early phase under examination. As is well known, many negative and non-negative sentences produced at this time contain null subjects. Recall that *pro* subjects are hypothesized to be VP-internal subjects in the model of the grammar adopted here. This means that null subjects negatives, some examples of which are given in (4), should also be included in the count of negatives with VP-internal subjects.

(4)   Some null subject negatives

        a. can't open (Peter, 2–0–1)
        b. no ride a bike (Peter, 2–1–0)
        c. didn't come out (Peter, 2–1–3)

        d. no fit (Nina, 1–11–2)
        e. no come off? (Nina, 2–0–0)
        f. don't fit on the bottom shelf (2–0–0)

        g. can't push (Naomi, 1–9–3)
        h. don't like it (Naomi, 1–10–3)
        i. don't like this dinner (Naomi, 2–0–0)

        j. no going away (Eve, 1–8–2)
        k. not have coffee (Eve, 1–9–2)
        l. not giving papa this one (Eve, 1–10–0)

As seen in the tables in (5), adding null subjects to this tabulation causes a more unified developmental pattern across all four children to emerge. Since *pro* subjects are analyzed as null VP-internal subjects, the first two columns of the tables in (5) are added together in determining the percentage of VP-internal vs. VP-external subjects. An overall decrease in VP-internal subjects is then observed in all four children.

(5)

Eve's negatives

	TYPE of SUBJECT:		
	null	overt – [Spec, VP]	overt – [Spec, IP]
AGE			
1–8–0 to 1–9–2	6 +	9 (94%)	1 (6%)
1–11–0 to 2–0–2	8 +	1 (20%)	35 (80%)

Naomi's negatives

	TYPE of SUBJECT:		
	null	overt – [Spec, VP]	overt – [Spec, IP]
AGE			
1–9–1 to 1–10–0	2 +	0 (100%)	0 (0%)
2–0–1 to 2–1–3	7 +	0 (41%)	10 (59%)

Peter's negatives

	TYPE of SUBJECT:		
	null	overt – [Spec, VP]	overt – [Spec, IP]
AGE			
2–0–1 to 2–1–0	4 +	0 (100%)	0 (0%)
2–3–0 to 2–3–3	29 +	0 (74%)	10 (26%)

Nina's negatives

	TYPE of SUBJECT		
	null overt	– [Spec, VP]	overt – [Spec, IP]
AGE			
1–11–2 to 2–1–0	42 +	6 (100%)	0 (0%)
2–1–3 to 2–2–1	30 +	2 (55%)	26 (45%)

The percentages provided on the right-hand side of the tables in (5) simply indicate the proportion of negative sentences uttered during a given period which contain an overt subject in [Spec, IP] position, to the left of the negative element. For each child, this percentage increases as a function of age.

Let's now look at the clearcut cases of unraised subjects in more depth. Only two of the four children examined, Eve and Nina, produce a substantial number of nonanaphoric negatives with overt VP-internal subjects. Some examples of these are shown in (6):

(6)   Child negatives with VP-internal subjects

      a. no Mommy giving baby Sarah milk (Eve, 1–9–0)
      b not Fraser read it (Eve, 1–9–0)
      c. no Fraser drink all tea (Eve, 1–9–0)

      d. no my play my puppet. Play my toys (Nina, 2–0–2)
      e. no Mommy doing. David turn (Nina, 2–0–2)
      f. no lamb have it (Nina, 2–0–3)
      g. no lamb have a chair either (Nina, 2–0–3)
      h. don't dog stay in the room (Nina, 2–1–2)
      i. don't Nina get up (Nina, 2–1–2)
      j. no Leila have a turn (Nina, 2–1–3)
      k. not man up here on him head (2–2–1)

In examples (6d) and (6e), the contrast between the negative sentence and the child utterance which immediately follows it makes the nonanaphoric meaning of the negative clear. In all other instances, consideration of wider context was necessary to determine intended meaning. For each of the cases in (6), the context indicated nonanaphoric meaning and, therefore, nonanaphoric structure. The context of (6f-g) is given in (7) as illustration:

(7)   Context of utterances (6f-g)

      Mother: Can you put it on the floor?
      Nina: **No have it, Mommy.**

Mother: You don't want me to have it?
Nina: **No. No. No lamb have it. No lamb have it.**
Mother: You don't want the lamb to have it either.
Nina: **No lamb have a chair either.**

The phenomenon exemplified in (6) has typically been explained as a developmental stage of the grammar during which Neg resides outside the sentence proper, presumably in Comp (Klima and Bellugi, 1966; Bellugi, 1967; Bloom, 1970; Wode, 1977; Felix, 1987). In accord with the syntactic framework of the time, Bellugi characterized it as a stage prior to the acquisition of a transformation which lowers Neg from a position external to the sentence nucleus to a position inside the sentence. Based on a study of negative acquisition in German, Wode (1977), like Bloom (1970), claimed that all child negatives of the form Neg-Subject-V are anaphoric in meaning and therefore contain an external negative element. The fact that the relevant utterances tend to contain *no*, rather than the adult negative marker *not*, has often been taken as evidence for the view that young children have a syntactically distinct form of negation.

The Neg-in-Comp approach just described leads to the predictions (1) that *no* — as a sort of negative operator unique to child grammar, rather than as a variant of the adult negator *not* — should only surface in sentence-initial position, and (2) that child's grammar should generate sentences in which Neg is positioned to the left of modals and auxiliaries. As it turns out, neither of these expectations is fulfilled. Klima and Bellugi (1966) described a second stage in development of negative syntax as including sentences with subject NPs to the left of the negative. Among the examples they give are the following:

(8)   Evidence that *no* is not in Comp (Bellugi's Stage 2)

    a. he no bite you
    b. I no want envelope
    c. I no taste them

A look at additional data from four children shows that *no* appears inside the sentence both in the ungrammatical cases where it stands in for Aux+*not* or Aux+*n't* (9a, b) and in grammatical sentences where it serves as a modifier (9c-f):

(9)   Further evidence that *no* is not in Comp

    a. me no go home (Peter, 2–1–3)
    b. I no want go home (Peter, 2–2–1)
    c. you have no more dogs (Nina, 2–2–0)
    d. no balloons . . . I find no balloons (Naomi, 1–11–2)
    e. Cramer have no pocket (Eve, 1–9–2)
    f. there no squirrels (Eve, 1–11–0)

In both construction types, *no* appears in a position other then the beginning of the sentence. This casts doubt on the claim that *no* is generated in Comp in child language. The data in (8) and (9a, b), in particular, indicate that the child's choice of phonological form for the negator is not syntactically relevant. That French children almost never substitute *non* (no) for *pas* (not) suggests that the correct explanation for this substitution in English concerns phonological-articulatory development (Deprez and Pierce, in press).

The second prediction of the Neg-in-Comp hypothesis, that the child's grammar will generate sentences of the form Neg-Subject-Aux-V or Neg-Aux-Subject-V, does not appear to be borne out by the data either. I found only one child utterance in which Neg precedes an auxiliary element ("No Butch is gonna walk" Peter, 2–2–1). Yet there are numerous early child utterances in which Aux precedes Neg. The vast majority of these contain the contracted forms *don't* and *can't*, as in some of the examples with null and internal subjects included in (5) and (6). Similar findings in the acquisition of French negation, as discussed below in this chapter, provide an even stronger case against the view that the two-year old's syntax of negation is fundamentally distinct from that of the adult.

If Neg is not in Comp in the immature grammar of English, then where is it? I suggest that it is internal to the sentence, in the same position is occupies in the adult grammar, between Infl and VP. This means that any subject occurring to the right of a negative element is located within VP. Early child utterances of the type in (4) and (6), therefore, are readily described in current syntactic theory as containing VP-internal subjects.

The proposed analysis of this long-studied construction in English child language is depicted in (10):

(10)   S-structure of child utterance (6e)

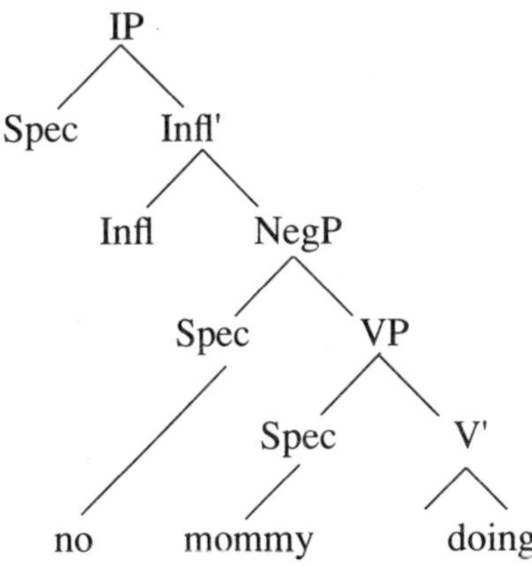

As in the adult grammar, the child's negative *no* is located in [Spec, NegP] position.[4] Unlike the adult, however, the child leaves the subject in VP-internal position, presumably because the immature grammar does not force the raising of subjects for Case reasons. In this way, the child language phenomenon of sentence-initial negation constitutes powerful support for the VP-internal subject hypothesis (see also Lebeaux, 1988).

It is obvious from (5) that children make widespread use of a mechanism of subject raising before the age of two and a half years. Since the initial-state grammar is hypothesized to be one which does not require the subject to raise out of VP-internal position, we are faced with the question what triggers subject raising. Simple subject-verb-object sentences in the English input provide no clue to the child that subject raising has taken place, if indeed it has. But sentences containing overt material within Infl, such as negative markers and auxiliaries, are exactly the environment that makes subject raising explicit. I therefore propose negatives and noninterrogative sentences containing modals and auxiliaries, which are discussed in the next chapter, as candidates for the triggering experience in this domain.[5] That is, these constructions, which are undoubtedly abundant in the input, cause the child acquiring English to reset the relevant parameter to the value which forces subject raising, at least in certain structural contexts. Chapter 7 elaborates on this, when I further consider the analysis of subject raising in the adult grammar.

By way of leading into the discussion of French, let's consider one more fact about English acquisition. It is generally taken for granted that youngsters acquiring English fail to make gross errors in basic word order. In chapter 2, I showed that this generalization holds of the ordering of subjects and verbs, with the exception of some unaccusative constructions. This was seen to contrast with the very variable placement of subjects in French. I have shown in this chapter that a small number of word order errors in the development of English arise in the domain of negation. In these instances, some children produce ungrammatical sentences in which the subject follows the negative element. Yet we do not observe utterances in which the negative is placed incorrectly with respect to an auxiliary element. Nor do we generally observe ungrammatical ordering of main verbs and negators. That children correctly stop short of producing sentences in which the verb precedes the negative elements indicates that they have correctly set the parameter which excludes main verb raising in English but which allows it in French. This observation gains import when compared to the French acquisition data on negation and verb raising.

3.2 NEGATION IN FRENCH CHILD LANGUAGE

3.2.1 Comparative findings

As with English, the model of the grammar I have adopted predicts an early stage in the acquisition of French in which markers of negation surface in sentence-initial position. This prediction holds under the assumption that the child's grammar does not force raising of the subject and verb. If it is discovered that two-year old speakers of French produce comparatively few Neg-initial constructions, then it is because either the subject or the verb (or both) raises obligatorily. In order to distinguish among these possibilities, I will examine the position of the subject relative to negation separately from that of the verb relative to negation.

Ignoring the position of the verb for the time being, it is observed that NP subjects in the negative sentences of child French almost never appear in [Spec, IP] position. This is comparable to the early stage in English acquisition discussed just above. Unlike in the case of English, however, the French data do not exhibit an extreme shift in relative proportion of internal and external NP subjects. Throughout the period examined, children produced few negatives with NP subjects in sentence-initial position, but many with NP subjects in non-initial position.[6] As shown in the tables in (11), there is limited developmental change in the expected direction, with the exception of one child (Grégoire), in the proportion of external and internal subjects:

(11)

Philippe's negatives

| | | TYPE of SUBJECT: | | |
	null	overt – [Spec, VP]		overt – [Spec, IP]
AGE				
2–1–3 to 2–2–1	30 +	8	(95%)	2 (5%)
2–2–2 to 2–3–0	15 +	3	(90%)	2 (10%)

Grégoire negatives

	null		TYPES of SUBJECT: overt – [Spec, VP]		overt – [Spec, IP]
AGE					
1–9–2 to 2–0–1	11	+	2	(93%)	1 (7%)
2–1–3 to 2–3–0	27	+	1	(97%)	1 (3%)

Nathalie's negatives

	null		TYPE of SUBJECT: overt – [Spec, VP]		overt – [Spec, IP]
AGE					
1–9–3 to 2–1–1	53	+	52	(99%)	1 (1%)
2–2–2 to 2–3–2	31	+	10	(87%)	6 (13%)

Daniel's negatives

	null		TYPE of SUBJECT: overt – [Spec, VP]		overt – [Spec, IP]
AGE					
1–8–1 to 1–10–2	65	+	7	(99%)	1 (1%)
1–11–1	16	+	2	(90%)	2 (0%)

Overt VP-internal subjects do not disappear as they did in English. As discussed in chapter 2, postverbal subjects remain common in spoken adult French. The proportion of overt subjects which are VP-internal nonetheless declines for each child during the relevant period: for Philippe, it drops from 80% to 50%; for Grégoire, from 67% to 50%; for Nathalie, from 98% to 63%; for Daniel, from 80% to 50%. This reflects an increase in subject raising from one period to the next. Raised subjects account for 5% (16 out of 305 utterances) of the data on French negation, while unraised overt subjects account for 27% (82 of 305). Overall, the proportion of VP-internal subjects, null and overt, remains quite large, in contrast to the decrease observed in English. Some examples of overt, arguably VP-internal, subjects under negation are provided in (12):

(12)   French negatives with VP-internal subjects

a. pas la poupée dormir (Nathalie, 1–9–3)
   (not the doll$_{subj}$ sleep$_{inf}$)

b. pas manger la poupée (Nathalie, 1–9–3)
   (not eat$_{inf}$ the doll$_{subj}$)

c. fait pas du bruit la fille (Philippe, 2–2–0)
   (makes not noise the girl$_{subj}$)

d. écris pas moi (Philippe, 2–2–1)
   (write not me$_{subj}$)

e. a plus papa (Grégoire, 1–9–2)
   (has no more papa$_{subj}$)

f. non est grande pomme de terre (Grégoire, 2–1–3)
   (no is big the apple$_{subj}$)

g. pleure pas garçon (Daniel, 1–8–1)
   (cries not boy$_{subj}$)

h. plus jouer tracteur bébé (Daniel, 1–8–3)
   (no more play$_{inf}$ tractor baby$_{subj}$)

The utterance in (12f) represents the only instance I found in which *non* (*no*), rather than *pas* (*not*), is used by a French child to negate a sentence. The near absence of this construction type confirms that the use of *no* in English does not reflect a universal first stage in the acquisition of negation. All other cases in (12) in which the negative appears in sentence-initial position contain nonfinite verbs. This is representative of the placement of Neg overall in the French data.

Although NP subjects tend not to occur in initial position, the prediction of an early stage in the acquisition of negation during which negators are generally sentence-initial, paralleling English development, is in some sense not borne out. This is because finite verbs often appear in initial position, to the left of the negatives themselves. In short, French children as young as 20 months of age demonstrate knowledge and use of verb raising. (13) contains examples of verb placement in finite and nonfinite negatives:

(13) French data showing that +/– finite determines location of Neg

[−infinite]	[+finite]
a. pas manger (Nathalie 1–9–3) (*not eat*)	b. veux pas lolo (Nathalie 2–0–1) (*want not water*)
c. pas casser (Daniel 1–8–1) (*not break*)	d. marche pas (Daniel 1–8–3) (*works not*)
e. pas rouler en vélo (Philippe 2–2–1) (*not roll on bike*)	f. ça tourne pas (Philippe 2–1–3) (*this turns not*)
no relevant examples	g. elle roule pas (Grégoire 1–11–3) (*it doesn't roll*)

3.2.2 Negative placement as evidence for Infl

The contingency in French between finiteness and verb placement relative to negation is considered a primary source of evidence for the role of verb movement to Infl in French syntax (Emonds, 1978; Pollock, 1989). Since the same contingency is observed in child French, there is little doubt that very young French children have verb raising. A more interesting implication of this contingency from the acquisition perspective, however, is the presence of Infl. As was first pointed out by Weissenborn (1988a), the fact that tensed verbs move to a position to the left of the negative in early French syntax indicates that Infl is available as a landing site for the moved verb. This observation forms a central argument in the case against the claim that early grammar is best characterized at Infl-less or as lacking in functional projections altogether (cf. Guilfoyle and Noonan, 1988; Kazman, 1988; Aldridge, 1988; Radford, 1990).

The contingency between verb placement and finiteness is evident in each of the four children, as illustrated in the tables in (14):

(14)   Verb placement in negatives as a function of tense

Philippe

	+FINITE	−FINITE
verb-Neg	52	1
Neg-verb	3	4

Grégoire

	+FINITE	−FINITE
verb-Neg	43	0
Neg-verb	0	0

Nathalie

	+FINITE	−FINITE
verb-Neg	68	0
Neg-verb	3	82

Daniel

	+FINITE	−FINITE
verb-Neg	53	1
Neg-verb	3	36

Of 352 negative utterances, only 11 (or 3%) fail to conform to the grammatical generalization that finite verbs occur to the left of the negative and nonfinite verbs occur to the right of the negative. Furthermore, all four children measured individually demonstrate equally significant contingencies (in Chi-square tests) along the appro-

priate lines between verb placement and tense (p <. 001). This proves
that the placement of the verb with respect to the negative element is
far from arbitrary. Since it depends on the finiteness of the verb, it
must be that the grammar of the very young child represents finiteness
and a projection of Infl into which the tensed verb can move. This
issue is explored further in the next chapter.

3.3 COMPARATIVE SUMMARY

The finite/nonfinite distinction instantiated in (13) and (14) serves as a
firm indication that there is "knowledge of Infl" in the minds of very
young children. That this distinction is readily perceived in the examination of early French but not in that of early English does not mean
that the Infl projection is lacking in the latter. It merely demonstrates
the importance of crosslinguistic surveys of acquisition when trying to
characterize the early grammar. In comparing the French and English
findings, a telling difference emerges. Young speakers of English, but
not young speakers of French, pass through a fairly clear-cut phase of
negative development in which the negative marker tends to surface
exclusively in sentence-initial position. This was attributed to the
underlying VP-internal structure and lack of subject raising. What dis-
tinguishes child English from child French in this domain, then, is the
verb-raising parameter. French makes use of main verb raising and
English does not. That young children have set this parameter correctly is demonstrated by the lack of English utterances such as "want
not water" and the plenitude of French utterances like "veux pas lolo"
in (13b).

As a further consequence of this analysis, the dearth of subject
raising observed during the early period cannot simply be attributed to
the absence of the Infl projection. As indicated by the availability of
verb movement, the Infl node is clearly projected. Early verb movement also argues against the view, challenged earlier in this chapter,
that Neg is generated in Comp in the grammar of the young child.
Since the verb raises into Infl on the left of Neg, Neg must reside

below Infl. In short, Neg is situated in the same position in child and adult grammars.

NOTES

[1] The discussion in this chapter reflects work done in collaboration with V. Deprez. In particular, see Deprez and Pierce (in press).

[2] Both examples in (2) are found in the on-line CHILDES transcripts of the child Adam's speech (Brown, 1973; MacWhinney and Snow, 1985).

[3] While the successive speech samples considered for each child were selected in order to show the changing distribution of the relevant structures, they also break down roughly into according to MLU, with the first sample in each case culled from transcripts with an MLU of 2 to 3 morphemes and the second sample culled from transcripts with an MLU of 3 to 4 morphemes.

[4] Equivalently, following Zanuttini (1989), *no* here may be a VP-adjunct, a proposal that responds to the objection that Neg in the Spec of NegP may function as a barrier to Infl-government of the VP and its specifier.

[5] Note that these construction types readily meet simple learnability requirements, such as Lightfoot's (1991) degree-0 learnability, since they contain no embedded clauses and occur very frequently.

[6] Note, as described in chapter 5, that pronominal subjects are accorded a clitic analysis and therefore do not count towards calculations involving the distribution of NP subjects. Rather, sentences with only pronominal subjects are counted here as null subjects.

CHAPTER 4

INFLECTIONAL AFFIXATION

In this chapter, English and French acquisition are contrasted in the domain of inflectional affixation. The theoretical model discussed earlier, in particular the claim that French grammar includes main verb raising and English grammar does not, leads to the expectation of differing developmental patterns. And, as discussed in previous chapters, there is evidence for just such a difference in the appropriate early setting of the verb raising parameter.

In chapter 1, I reviewed the literature on verb raising to Infl which establishes that all finite verbs undergo raising in French, but only *be* and auxiliary *have* raise out of the VP in the syntax of English. Main verbs are inflected in syntax via the mechanism of affix lowering. On Pollock's (1989) account, verbs that assign thematic roles are prevented from raising to Infl in English because properties of inflection in English block theta transmission. Since *be* and auxiliary *have* do not assign thematic roles, raising to Infl does not result in a violation of the theta criterion. Inflectional affixation in English, then, is accomplished by raising to Infl in the case of *be* and auxiliary *have*, and by affix lowering into VP in the case of all other verbs.

The child acquiring English is typically over three years of age when he masters the system of verbal inflection in his language (Brown, 1973; Pinker, 1984; Guilfoyle, 1984; Hyams and Jaeggli, 1988, among others). How is the absence of overt inflectional markers in early English to be interpreted? Many have used this observation to argue that the early grammar is best characterized as lacking an inflectional system (Guilfoyle and Noonan, 1988; Kazman, 1989; Radford, 1990). While this view accounts for superficial properties of two year-old English speech, it does not account for more subtle distributional facts in English, nor for crosslinguistic patterns in inflectional development, both of which reveal early knowledge of a finite-nonfinite distinction. I first consider the early inflectional system of English. I then turn to French acquisition, where there is incontrovertible evidence that Infl forms part of the pre-two year-old grammar.

4.1 THE ACQUISITION OF VERBAL INFLECTION IN ENGLISH

4.1.1 Affix-lowering

There are a number of reports in the literature to the effect that the child acquiring English is slow to achieve productive inflectional affixation. This stands in contrast to the earlier acquisition of inflectional morphology in languages which have more complex systems for overt marking of tense and agreement (see Hyams, 1984). According to Brown's (1973) ranking of the acquisition order of 14 grammatical morphemes in three children, productive appropriate use of the past and third person regular morphemes is late, ranking nine and ten respectively. Brown's success criterion of 90% occurrence of a morpheme in required syntactic contexts is not achieved for *-ed* and *-s*, based on the childeren that he studied, until sometime after the age of three years. These overall results were replicated by deVilliers and deVilliers (1973) in a cross-sectional study of the acquisition of grammatical morphemes. In contrast, the present progressive morpheme *-ing* is acquired fairly early on, ranking first in the order of acquisition, both by Brown (1973) and deVilliers and deVilliers (1973).

While the *-ing* facts may be thought to show that a mechanism that attaches inflectional affixes to verbs is available from the start in English acquisition, there are reasons for believing that *-ing* does not undergo syntactic affixation in the adult or the child grammar. That is, it seems that the progressive participle is a base generated form, such that it is not represented at syntactic levels as an analyzed stem + affix. Rather, it is derived in the morphology (cf. also Hyams, 1986b). Emonds (1985) argues at length for the existence of what he terms bare VPs in English, non-NP gerunds that are not immediately dominated by an S-node. On Emonds' account, these include what is normally called the progressive form as well as other gerundive forms, such as the reduced relative (e.g. *They burned a box containing books*) and adverbial gerunds (e.g. *John always studies chemistry using my notebooks*). Based on the syntactic distribution of this class of elements, namely as nonfinite complements to verbs, Emonds argues that they do not undergo inflectional affixation. Rather, this form of the verb is thought to be a direct morphological realization of a base structure. There are thus independent arguments in the linguistic literature for assuming base generation of the progressive participle.

Another argument for the base generation of the progressive participle comes directly from the child language data. Simply to say that the progressive surfaces early falls short of characterizing the extent of their usage in early child language. These forms, without the required auxiliary *be*, are used in abundance by some children at early stages. For the child Naomi, for example, 23% of all main verbs produced during the young period I examined contain the progressive ending. This percentage is also quite high for Nina (16%) and Eve (14%). Of the four children, the only child to produce few progressive forms in the age range under consideration is Peter (3%). Furthermore, verbs in the progressive form distribute with null, pronominal and lexical subjects, and are just as likely to occur with an overt subject as the root form of the verb (see chapter 6). If it is maintained that the child who can utter only two to three words in sequence will avoid unnecessary morphemes, it is even more difficult to account for this rate of occurrence without positing that *-ing* does not count as an independent morpheme, i.e. that progressives are base generated. Also of interest are the many overtensing errors with auxiliaries made by children at this stage which involve the progressive participle (Pinker, 1984). This further suggests that these participles are unanalyzed, base generated forms. In sum, the claim the inflectional affixation is slow to be acquired in English child language is not challenged by the fact of early progressives, as the latter do not appear to entail syntactic derivational affixation.[1]

Viewed from the perspective of the input, the late acquisition of certain inflectional morphemes in English is really not surprising. In particular, the lateness of the third person singular marker -*s* is exactly as one might expect based on the nature of spoken English. Indeed, the simple present tense is rare in spoken English (Campbell, 1991). Unless it is intended to describe habitual activity, a sentence such as *Ed goes to the store* is generally avoided. Instead, the progressive *Ed is going to the store* is used. It is therefore very likely that an examination of parental speech would show that the input contains a relatively small number of verbs ending in third person singular -*s*. The earlier acquisition of the progressive morpheme than of the third person singular morpheme, then, is predicted to a certain (as yet unspecified) extent by the nature of the input.

But there is another explanation for delays in the acquisition of English inflectional morphology that I would like to consider. This concerns derivational economy. As outlined in chapter 1, there are actually two accounts in the derivational economy mode which lead to the prediction of delays in the acquisition of English verbal inflection. The affixation of inflectional endings in English results from affix-lowering. Following Chomsky (1988), where it is argued that affix lowering is more costly in derivational terms than verb raising, and assuming generally that derivational economy constrains the acquisition process, late emergence of productive inflectional affixation in English is predicted. The other account, from Hyams (1984), goes as follows: core phenomena are acquired earlier than peripheral phenomena; verbal inflectional morphology is peripheral in English; hence, it is predicted that inflectional affixation will be acquired later in English than in languages with core (i.e. overtly articulated) inflectional morphology.

The absence of verbal inflection in early English speech has often been taken to indicate the lack of a capacity to represent inflection. Viewed on its own, however, the English child language data is misleading. The claim that the immature grammar lacks functional projections is especially difficult to maintain in the face of acquisition evidence from languages other than English. If the universal form of the initial-state grammar is construed as containing only lexical projections, then how is the early acquisition of inflectional morphology in languages with complex inflectional systems to be explained? Two prime examples are Italian and Polish. According to Hyams (1984), children acquiring Italian master the present tense verbal paradigm by about two years of age. Similarly, Weist *et al.* (1984) report that Polish children acquire productive control over subject-verb agreement by 21 months of age. Even in French, where the basic system of overt inflectional marking is relatively impoverished, there is clearcut evidence for early control over basic tense and agreement distinctions, as I discuss in section 4.2.

4.1.2 Auxiliaries and modals

Recall that, apart from the +/- verb raising distinction, another difference between the inflectional systems of English and French concerns the content of tensed inflection the two languages. While tensed Infl is always realized as an inflectional affix in French, English has a separate class of auxiliary elements, the modals, which are base generated in Infl (Roberts, 1985; Emonds, 1985). Emonds (1985) argues that the English modals form a word-class distinct from the class of verbs. In effect, English has two sets of inflectional elements, affixes and modals. Unlike modal verbs in French, which raise to Infl along with other verbs, modals in English are never situated within the verb phrase. The class of English modals, like the negatives, thus provides a test for the claim that early child language is characterized in part by VP-internal subjects. Unlike syntactic affixes, which are filtered out if they remain unbound, modals stand on their own. The model thus makes a prediction with respect to word order in the early production of modals and auxiliary verbs. Since modals are base generated in Infl, and auxiliaries raise to Infl, the child who is not always raising subjects to [Spec, IP] position, is expected to produce Aux-subject word order.[2]

There is indeed suggestive evidence to the effect that early constructions with Aux-subject order contain an unraised subject in VP-internal position. First of all, as soon as they are used, auxiliary verbs are found to be placed correctly in yes/no questions (Klima and Bellugi, 1966; Stromswold, 1990). Stromswold (1990) also reports early success at inverted word order in the vast majority of wh-questions. Turning to specific data, the tables in (1) display how auxiliaries and modals are positioned as a function of age in the four children. These tables are intended to parallel the Neg placement tables in (3) of the previous chapter.

(1)

Eve's Aux placement[3]

AGE	Aux-initial		Aux-medial
1–8–0 to 1–9–2	8	(73%)	3
1–11–0 to 2–0–2	19		31 (62%)

Naomi's Aux placement

AGE	Aux-initial		Aux-medial
1–9–1 to 1–10–0	0	(73%)	0
2–0–1 to 2–1–3	23	(73%)	7

Peter's Aux placement

AGE	Aux-initial		Aux-medial
2–0–1 to 2–1–0	2	(67%)	1
2–3–0 to 2–3–3	14	(54%)	12

Nina's Aux placement

AGE	Aux-initial	Aux-medial
1–11–2 to 2–1–0	4 (50%)	4
2–1–3 to 2–2–1	1	8 (89%)

For Eve and Nina, the same developmental shift is observed in the placement of negatives and the placement of non-negative auxiliaries: an early stage in which auxiliaries and negatives are often placed in initial position is followed by one in which they are more likely to be situated in sentence medial position. For Peter and Naomi, interestingly, the lack of a clear shift over the age range considered in the relative positioning of Aux parallels the lack of a clear shift in the relative positioning of negatives that was observed in the previous chapter. Although the correlation is far from exact, these parallels suggest that the same developing grammatical mechanism may be involved in the changing patterns in auxiliary and negative placement. According to the adopted syntactic framework, that mechanism is hypothesized to be subject raising. Unraised subjects are a defining characteristic of only the very early language.

Not to be overlooked in terms of evidence for the presence of Infl in the immature grammar is the simple fact that auxiliaries and negatives are used at a very young age by most children.[4] In addition, the absence of word order errors in which auxiliary verbs, modals and negatives are placed incorrectly with respect to the verb suggests that these elements are situated in Infl. As I mentioned in the previous chapter, the observation that the incorrect orderings Neg-Aux and main verb-Neg never occur shows both that Neg is not in Comp and that main verbs do not raise. Similarly, the fact that young children use auxiliaries and modals, placing them correctly with respect to the verb and with respect to negation, suggests that auxiliary verbs raise to Infl in English child language, that modals are generated in Infl and, in short, that Infl is present.

I turn now to a closer look at the positioning of auxiliaries in one child, Naomi, beginning with *be*.[5] The earliest occurrences of *be* reported in the literature are noncontractible tensed forms in sentences like *here it is* and *there it is* (Brown, 1973). Indeed, in the recorded speech of the child Naomi (Sachs, 1983) up to 22 months, is occurs in the following constructions:

(2)   a. There it is
        b. There is

It is clear from the discourse that these phrases serve a deictic function, yet they are not always used appropriately. Here is an example of a parent-child interchange:

(3)   Father: Where's the horsey? I don't see him.
        Naomi: There it is.
        Father: What's this?
        Naomi: **There it is, kitty.**

Many have argued, based on the contextual distribution of these phrases in child language, that they are rote learned units (cf. Bowerman, 1982; Peters, 1983). This is also usually assumed to be the correct analysis of early occurrences of contracted *be* in *that's, there's, here's* etc. Bellugi (1967) argues that pronoun + contractible *be* forms are merely surface variants of the pronouns themselves. The child does not analyze them into their component parts until a later stage.

In subsequent stages, still before two years of age, Naomi's utterances with *be* include those with *is* used appropriately in yes/no questions, wh-questions and as a copula:

(4)   a. is this doggie? (1–10–3)
        b. is it raining? (1–11–1)
        c. where is it? (1–10–2)
        d. is fixed (1–11–0)

    e. is broken (1–11–0)
    f. is empty (1–11–0)

Naomi is also using the plural form *are* at this time, in the constructions in (5):

(5)   a. are sheep running? (1–11–1)
       b. where are the more? (1–11–1)

Note that Naomi is using *be* both as a main verb copula and as an auxiliary, as in (4b) and (5a). Since *be* in both constructions undergoes raising to Infl, the distinction between the two is not a point of concern here. Actually, there are two potential analyses of *be* at this stage that are consistent with this framework. Either be has raised to Infl in these constructions, or it is generated in Infl along with the class of modals in English. The noteworthy fact about early use of is in constructions which appear to be structurally analyzed by the child is precisely that it occurs in sentence-initial position (with the exception of wh-words).

In the full period under examination, *is* almost always fails to appear with a subject to its left. Specifically, between the ages of 1–9–3 and 2–1–3 Naomi produced a total of 92 utterances with non-contracted *is*. Of these, 82 (89%) occur without a subject to the left, meaning that the subject was either omitted or unraised, or that the utterance was a question. Of the 10 exceptions, six contained *This is*, which may not be morphologically analyzed by the child. For purposes of illustration, in (6) are all utterances containing is produced in a single speech sample taped at 1–11–1:

(6)   a. is toaster (uttered twice)
       b. is it raining? (uttered twice)
       c. is locked?
       d. is locked (uttered 3 times)
       e. is it gone? (uttered twice)
       f. is it going to work?
       g. is he going to work? (uttered 4 times)
       h. how big is

The same generalization holds of Naomi's early use of modals. Before the age of two, Naomi uses *can and could* only in yes/no questions and declaratives with empty subjects. (7) lists all of Naomi's utterances with can from 1–11–1 through 1–11–3:

(7)   a. can take it (uttered 3 times)
        b. can I get down? (uttered 4 times)
        c. can I get up?
        d. can climb it (uttered 5 times)
        e. can stand up
        f. can eat it
        g. can lie down (uttered twice)
        h. can do this?
        i. can do this!
        k. can I read this book? (uttered twice)
        l. can use this? (uttered twice)
        m. can make fish?
        n. can make that (uttered twice)
        o. can make it
        p. can make tail
        q. can drink cocoa
        r. can drink it? (uttered 3 times)
        s. can drink coffee
        t. can eat nana

Of the 50 utterances with nonnegated *can* produced during the total period studied, only three contain a subject to the left of the modal. As I will show in chapter 6, the rate of null subjects alone does not account for the absence of overt subjects in initial position of sentences containing auxiliaries or modals.

Even more impressive from the standpoint of model's prediction that early grammar will be found to contain unraised VP-internal subjects, there is an interesting class of errors that the model predicts and that children appear to make. These involve faulty word order in declarative sentences with auxiliary verbs. In (8) are some examples, in discourse context, of these word errors in the speech of Naomi. (9)

contains a few similar examples from other children. In all of the utterances exemplified here, the AUX element occurs in initial position in what is intended as an affirmative sentence. In each case, the transcripts explicitly did not identify the utterance as having been produced with question intonation.

(8)   a. Father: Naomi, do uou want an egg?
         Naomi: **No, is it broke.**
         F: What? The ice is broken? What is broken Naomi?
         N: **Is it fixed.**
         F: Is it fixed?
         N: **Is fixed, is broken.**
         F: The ice isn't broken Naomi.

      b. Mother: Look at the shoes.
         Naomi: **Is shoes off.** Shoes shoes shoes
         M: What about it? Yes, those are shoes.

      c. Mother: Yes, you can have some bread, honey.
         Naomi: **Is that Nomi's.** Want that [!] dinner.
         M: Want that kind of dinner, too?

      d. Naomi: **Is kitty sleep.**
         Mother: Is kitty asleep?

      e. Naomi: Is.
         Father: What, Naomi?
         N: **Is it hard.**
         F: Yes, it is hard. Is it hard?

      f. Mother: Hey, Naomi, what's this?
         Naomi: **Is it, flowers.**

(9)   a. Adult : What I like best were the monkeys.
         Nina: **. . . Was monkeys climb on that balloon.**

      b. Nina: Is that your house.

c. Nina: Is the giraffe, mine.

d. Adult: It's Goldilocks. Is it? (Brown, 1973)
    Adam: **Yep, is it, Goldilocks.**

e. Adam   Do you drink it.
    Comment: Seems to be a statement.

f. Situation: (Peter sees adult look at the tape recorder)
    Peter: Is that tape, right Patsy?

g. Peter: Can we do it (no rising intonation)

h. Adult: So Lois can see.
    Peter: Lois xxx see.
    Adult: That's Lois. Uhhuh.
    Peter: Help. go zoom. **Can Lois xxx** see.

i. Peter: Here are they.

There are likely to be more of these Aux-initial utterances intended as declaratives in the child language transcripts, but it is not usually possible to identify these cases without access to detailed conversational context. Ideally, of course, we would like to have intonational information about these utterances. Yet careful study of existing transcripts is likely to unveil similar errors with other auxiliary elements. Errors such as these are expected only if the subject generated in VP-internal position fails to raise.

The analysis I propose for utterances in (8) and (9) is as in (10):

(10)   S-structure for utterance (8c)

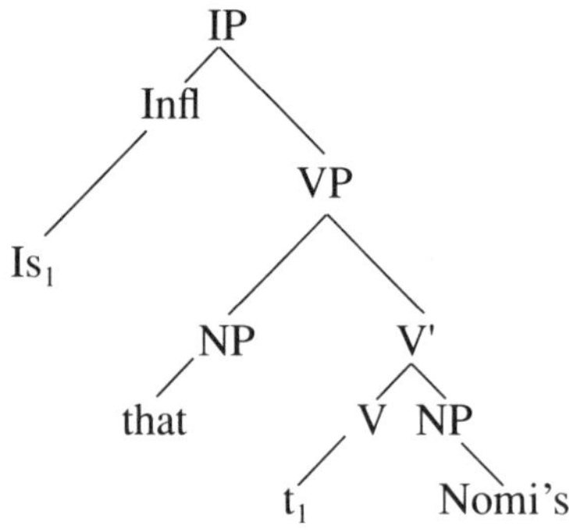

By hypothesis, the child's grammar does not force raising of the VP-internal subject. In Deprez and Pierce (in press), we extend this analysis to the early acquisition of subject-Aux inversion in questions. That is, we attribute Aux-subject word order in yes/no and wh-questions in the two-year old grammar to the structure in (11). Based largely on German child language which indicates a delay in the acquisition of verb raising to Comp, we suggest that all Aux-subject order at the early stages, even in questions, results from unraised VP-internal subjects and the fact that auxiliaries reside in Infl.

In sum, the existence of a stage in English child language in which inflectional material occurs predominantly on the left periphery of the sentence provides support for the grammatical model assumed here. Modals are generated in Infl, tensed auxiliaries raise to Infl and the subject is generated within the VP, while the derivational process of subject raising which permutes this underlying configuration is not fully acquired.[6] As evidence for the existence of an Infl system in the early grammar, it was observed that young children actually produce negatives and auxiliaries, which are assumed to reside in Infl, at a very young age. It was also observed that they place these for the most part correctly, but occasionally produce revealing errors in which auxiliary items are positioned to the left of the overt subject in a declarative. This explicitly parallels the type of word order errors observed in early negative sentences.

The fact that children acquring English use auxiliaries, modals and negatives and place them appropriately was taken to show early representation of an inflectional system. When it comes to presenting evidence for knowledge of the verbal inflectional system, there are really two separate types of behavior to consider, apart from the fact that Infl, functional category, is instantiated at all in the early vocabulary: (1) use of distinctive morphological forms, and (2) correct positioning of inflectional elements relative to each other and relative to the verb. In considering French, I will first examine knowledge of certain distinct inflectional elements and then look at how these elements are positioned.

4.2 THE ACQUISITION OF VERBAL INFLECTION IN FRENCH

4.2.1 Background

Regular verbs with the infinitive *-er* ending make up roughly 90% of all French verbs (Dietiker, 1978). The present tense indicative conjugation of this common verb type is illustrated in (11), using the verb *parler* (to speak):

(11)　　　first person singular:　**je parle**
　　　　　　　　　　　plural:　**nous parlons**

　　　　second person singular:　**tu parles**
　　　　　　　　plural/formal:　**vous parlez**

　　　　third person singular:　**il, elle, on parle**
　　　　　　　　　　　plural:　**ils, elles parlent**

The bolded inflectional endings of the first, second and third person singular and the third person plural are not pronounced. Therefore, the verb in all four cases, although spelled differently, is pronounced alike. The two overtly distinctive forms, the first and second person plural, occur relatively infrequently in the spoken language, as it is now common to use the impersonal *on parle* (one speaks) in place of *nous parlons* (we speak). From the child's perspective, then, there may be only one form of the verb for the regular present tense. This means that young children can typically demonstrate knowledge of the verbal agreement paradigm only through their use of subject clitic pronouns. As I discuss at length in the next chapter, subject pronouns in French are arguably syntactic clitics, generated in Infl or Agr and on their way (in the diachronic sense) to becoming obligatory verbal affixes.

4.2.2 The instantiation of Infl

Let's consider, then, French children's acquisition of the personal subject pronouns *je* (I), *tu* (you), *il(s)* (he, they or it), *elle(s)* (she, they or it) and *on* (one). (12) below charts the emergence of these common pronouns in the four children, based on first appearance in available transcripts.

(12)   Age of first pronoun use

Grégoire
il(s)   (1–9–2)
elle(s)   (1–10–0)
je   (1–10–0)
on   (1–10–0)
tu   (2–1–3)

Philippe[7]
il(s)   (2–1–3)
elle(s)   (2–1–3)
je   (2–1–3)
on   (2–1–3)
tu   (2–1–3)

Nathalie
elle(s)   (1–10–2)
il(s)   (2–2–2)
je   (2–2–2)
on   (2–2–2)
tu   not in evidence by 2–2–2

Daniel
elle(s)   (1 8–1)
je   (1–8–1)
on   (1–8–1)
il(s)   (1–8–3)
tu   not in evidence by 1–11–1

Assuming that the age of Philippe at first use of these pronouns is actually somewhat younger (see footnote 7), three of the four children are marking agreement productively before or about the age of two. The exception is the child Nathalie, whose first pronoun occurs at (1–10–2) although she doesn't appear to use more than one subject pronoun form until four months later. This may be artifact of her tendency to collapse the subject pronouns *il* and *elle* and the auxiliaries *est* (is) and *a* (has) into a single form *la*. This early use of personal subject pronouns strongly suggests access to an inflectional system for marking agreement. In particular, under the analysis that these pronominal forms are actually generated in Infl (see chapter 5), it shows that Infl is in fact represented and generated.

There is another way in which young French children distinctively mark for infection, by differentiating finite and nonfinite verbal forms. As illustrated in (13), which contains only a few of the many relevant examples, all four children use both finite and nonfinite forms of the same verbs.

(13)   Children's use of both + and − finite forms of verbs

Philippe

2–2–2: a. pas rouler en vélo   elle roule
           (*not roll on the bike*)   (*it rolls*)
2–2–2: b. pour rentrer là la voiture   il rentre
           (*for re-entering there the car*) (*it re-enters*)

Nathalie

2–2–2: c. train va tomber   tombe
           (*train is going to fall*)   (*falls*)
2–2–2: d. voir l'auto papa   elle la vois l'auto
           (*to see papa's car*)   (*she it sees the car*)

Daniel

1–11–1: e. veut dormir bébé   dort bébé
           (*wants to sleep baby*)   (*sleeps baby*)
1–11–1: f. je vais faire café moi   fait la vaisselle
           (*I'm going to make coffee*)   (*does the dishes*)

Grégoire

1–10–0: g. mangé le chien   il mange
           (*ate the dog*)   (*he eats*)
1–11–3: h. est passé dans la rue   elle passe
           (*passed in the street*)   (*it passes*)

Data like that in (13) show that the child's choice of verbal form even at this young age is other than arbitrary. That is, they are not simply using one rote-learned form for every verbal lexical entry.

Not surprisingly, it was found that children's overall use of finite as opposed to nonfinite forms increases with age. This is illustrated in (14):

(14)   Proportion of verbs which are finite

Grégoire
G1 (1–9–2)   70% (26/37)
G2 (1–10–0)   51% (59/116)
G3 (1-10-3)   61% (43/70)
G4 (1–11–3)   77% (76/99)
G5 (2–0–1)   51% (49/96)
G6 (2–1–3)   81% (35/43)
G7 (2–3–0)   89% (69/78)

Nathalie
N1 (1–9–3)   4% (3/81)
N2 (1–10–1)   29% (31/108)
N4 (2–0–1)   34% (26/76)
N6 (2–2–2)   54% (70/129)
N7 (2–3–2)   90% (152/168)

Daniel
D1 (1–8–1)   40% (42/104)
D2 (1–8–3)   41% (53/128)
D3 (1–9–3)   41% (55/133)
D4 (1–10–2)   58% (125/217)
D5 (1–11–1)   78% (156/199)

Philippe
P1 (2–1–3)   79% (65/93)
P2 (2–2–0)   76% (135/177)
P3 (2–2–1)   86% (115/134)
P4 (2–2–2)   65% (69/107)
P7 (2–3–0)   71% (81/114)

Philippe is exceptional in this regard because he is already using a high percentage of finite verbs at the time of the initial recording. With the exception of Nathalie's first transcript, all children at all ages use a substantial proportion of tensed verbs. This suggests that verb raising is available from the onset of syntactic development. In fact, it is quite possible that many of the nonfinite verbs observed are an artifact of the tendency to drop the auxiliary verb from periphrastic constructions.

Quite impressively, however, children use these distinctively marked forms in an appropriate, nonrandom manner. This brings me from the most obvious type of inflectional knowledge found in early speech — the instantiation of inflectional categories — to the second, more subtle form of knowledge of verbal inflection that a young child can demonstrate, namely correct positioning of inflected and inflectional elements relative to one another.

4.2.3 Relative positioning of inflectional elements

As we saw in the previous chapter, verbs are positioned to the right of the negative marker when in the infinitive, but to the left of the negative marker when finite. This is an extremely significant result for all four children measured individually ($p < 0.001$). The same holds of the placement of finite and nonfinite verbs with respect to another inflectional element, namely the subject clitic. As I mentioned, I am assuming that agreement in spoken French takes overt form in the subject clitic. In order to evaluate both this assumption and the child's access to functional categories, it is necessary to examine how finite and nonfinite verbs are positioned relative to subject clitics. As it turns out, the contingency in this domain is just as striking as in the case of negation. (16) lists the number of subject clitic pronouns occurring in tensed and untensed clauses.

(16)   Occurrence of subject pronouns as a function of tense
         ($t = 4.57, p < 0.025$)

	+ FINITE	− FINITE
Philippe	196 (99%)	3
Grégoire	143 (98%)	3
Nathalie	162 (96%)	7
Daniel	104 (88%)	14

From 88 to 99% of all subject clitics, depending upon the child, occur in overtly tensed clauses. This leaves a total of only 27 (or less than 5%) exceptions to the generalization that subject clitics distribute exclusively with finite verbs. This is a very strong indication that these children represent finiteness. But it also reveals something about the nature of the subject clitic pronouns themselves. That they are excluded in nonfinite clauses suggests that they require a finite verb that raises to Infl to cliticize onto. I return to this analysis of subject pronouns in the next chapter.

Models of acquisition which propose that there are no functional categories at early stages are forced to claim that any early inflectional items are either unanalyzed by the child or structurally represented in a manner specific to child language (see Radford, 1990). My position here, in contrast, is that inflectional material is structurally represented in the young child's grammar exactly as it is in the adult grammar (at least at the level of D-structure). This parallelism between child and adult grammar was argued for at length in the case of the position of negation in English and French. And, in the case of subject pronouns in French, it is further developed in the next chapter. In this chapter, I have argued that the subject clitic-tense contingency constitutes further evidence that children have "knowledge of Infl" and indeed have functional categories.

Given these two extreme contingencies, that between the placement of negation and verb tense and that between the occurrence of subject pronouns and verbal tense, it is not possible to conclude that the immature grammar lacks an inflectional system, as, for example, (Radford 1990), claims. In fact, these contingencies demonstrate rather elegantly how misleading superficial properties of child language, such as missing inflectional affixes in English, really are from the standpoint of the underlying grammar. The only way the young French child could get these generalizations right is via representation of an Infl system. In the case of negation, this representational knowledge leads the child to situate the verb to the left of the negative marker according to whether Infl is +finite. In the case of subject clitics, it leads the child to allow subject pronouns only in finite clauses; as an affix, the subject clitic is filtered out in the absence of a raised verb to attach to. If the subject clitic did not reside in Infl, then this contingency would not arise. If the subject clitic resides in Infl, as it appears to, then Infl itself must be represented in the very early grammar.

NOTES

[1] See Pierce (1989) for comparison of these facts to similar observations on the syntax and acquisition of Spanish.

[2] In a related analysis of adult English, Aux-Subject order in question inversion constructions is argued to be the base-generated order, where subject raising to [Spec, IP] is blocked because that position serves as the landing site for matrix wh-movement (Pesetsky, 1989).

[3] These tabulations consider non-negative auxiliaries only, as negatives were tabulated in the same fashion, according to the same age-ranges, in the previous chapter. Furthermore, only declaratives are considered. Note that for Peter and Nina, calculations exclude utterances beginning with *This is*, as this was clearly a rote-learned phrase, often used inappropriately by these two children, but not by Naomi and Eve.

[4] According to Newport, Gleitman and Gleitman (1977), auxiliaries and modals tend to appear quite early, but the course of their acquisition in individual children is dependent upon characteristics of maternal speech.

[5] The auxiliary *have* arises very late (Brown, 1973). Indeed, *have* is used exclusively as a main verb until more advanced stages in the development of American English and thus will not be considered here.

[6] It is of course conceivable that not all children will overtly pass through the stage described in this section. The child who acquires subject raising relatively early, for example, might not.

[7] 2–1–3 is the age of the earliest Philippe transcript. Based on the fact that various subject pronouns were used quite productively in this initial speech sample, it can safely be assumed that these pronouns were first acquired some time earlier.

CHAPTER 5

PRONOMINAL SUBJECTS

The analysis of French subject pronouns as inflectional clitics as S-structure underlies my account of subject pronoun distribution in French child language mentioned in the previous chapter. This chapter compares the acquisition of subject pronouns in French and English. I claim that the comparative child language data support a syntactic distinction between subject pronouns in the two languages. While these pronominals behave as syntactic clitics in early French, they do not in early English. The acquisition data therefore serve as a surprising source of evidence for a particular analysis of these elements in the grammar of spoken French. The first section of this chapter gives some background on this issue. I then return to French child language, further examining the behavior of subject pronouns. Finally, patterns in the distribution of these pronouns in French are shown to contrast with the distribution of subject pronouns in English child language.

5.1 BACKGROUND ISSUES

The status of the class of subject pronouns in French known as weak forms (*je, tu, il, elle, nous, vous, ils, elles, on, ce*) is controversial. Kayne (1975) and Jaeggli (1982), for example, assert that these elements are syntactic clitics, lacking the status of independent morphemes at S-structure.[1] Others argue that while these elements may be clitics at the level of phonological form, they are in argument [Spec, IP] position in the syntax (e.g. Burzio, 1986; Rizzi, 1986b; Brandi and Cordin, 1989). I briefly review the arguments on both sides.

Jaeggli (1982), essentially following Kayne (1975), points to five environments in French syntax in which subject clitics behave differently from strong form pronouns and lexical subjects. First, nothing, with the exception of other clitics, can intervene between the subject clitic and the verb, even if demarcated by pauses:[2]

(1)   a. *Il, souvent, va au cinéma
           He/Jean, often, goes to the movies

        b. Jean, souvent, va au cinéma

Second, subject clitics cannot be conjoined, whereas lexical subjects can:

(2)   a. *Jean et je voulons aller au cinéma
           Jean and I want to go to the movies

        b. *Ils et elles veulent partir en vacances
           They (masc.) and they (fem.) want to take a vacation

        c. Jean et Marie veulent partir en vacances
           Jean and Marie want to take a vacation

Third, these clitics cannot be modified, whereas disjunctive (strong form) pronouns can:

(3)   a. *Ils tous partiront bientôt
           All of them will leave soon

        b. Eux tous partiront bientôt

Fourth, subject clitics are never contrastively stressed, whereas disjunctive pronouns are:

(4)   a. *Il partira le premier
           He will leave first

        b. Lui partira le premier

Finally, subject clitics do not occur in other NP positions:

(5)   a. *J'ai acheté ça pour tu
           I bought this for you

        b. J'ai acheté ça pour toi

Based on these observations, Jaeggli contends that subject clitics are not generated in subject position but rather in Infl, hence their obligatory closeness to the tensed verb.

Arguments to the opposite effect focus on a different set of facts, in which the behavior of subject clitics in French contrasts with that of subject clitics in certain Northern Italian dialects (e.g. Piedmontese, Trentino and Fiorentino). It has been argued that subject clitics in the Northern Italian dialects represent a spelling-out of agreement (Burzio, 1986; Rizzi, 1986b; Brandi and Cordin, 1989, among others). Among the central points raised against viewing subject pronouns in French in the same light are the following. First, while subject clitics co-occur with lexical subjects in the Italian dialects, they do not in standard French:[3]

(6)   a. Trentino: El Gianni el magna
                      John he eats

        b. French: *Jean il mange

Note the sentence in (6b) is only acceptable as a left dislocation, when it is pragmatically or intonationally marked as such. Second, while French subject clitics can be predicated of a conjunction of VPs, subject clitics in the dialects cannot; the subject clitic must be repeated in the second conjunct:

(7)   a. Trentino: La canta e la balla
                      She sings and she dances
        b. French: Elle chante et elle danse

        c. Trentino: *La canta e balla
                      She sings and dances

        d. French: Elle chante et danse

Third, subject clitics in French precede the negative clitic *ne*, while other clitics follow it. In contrast, the subject clitic in Trentino occurs to the right of the equivalent negative, *no*:[4]

(8)   a. Trentino: No la ghe l'ha dit
                       She has not said it to him

         b. French: Elle ne les aime pas/*Ne elle les aime pas
                       She doesn't like them

Finally, while the subject clitic is generally obligatory in the dialects, so that lexical subjects and clitics co-occur, lexical and clitic subjects in standard French are in complementary distribution. Compare (6) with (9):

(9)   a. Trentino: *El Gianni magna
                       Jean eats

         b. French: Jean mange

In chapter 7, I turn to a view of these facts in light of the distribution of subject clitics in spoken (or nonstandard) French, as discussed in the typological and functional linguistic literature. The description of subject clitics from this perspective shows them to be more closely aligned with subject clitics in the Italian dialects than is traditionally assumed. But my concern here is with the acquisition facts, and specifically with the question of how subject pronouns in early French child speech line up with respect to the potential analyses of subject pronouns I have just described.

5.2 SUBJECT PRONOUNS IN FRENCH CHILD LANGUAGE

In the previous chapter, I touched on the effects of the weak or clitic status of subject pronouns in French on the acquisition of inflection. In particular, it was found that subject pronouns were generated exclusively in the context of tensed verbs. This generalization accounts for over 95% (578 out of 605) of all utterances containing subject pronouns that were produced by the four children in the period under examination. As I have already said, this finding of a contingency between subject pronouns and finiteness is a very strong indication that the early grammar represents and projects Infl. But it also serves as an indication about the conditions under which subject pronouns are licensed. Since these pronominals only occur with tensed verbs, it may well be that they require the presence of tensed verbs to avoid being filtered out. On this view, they are syntactic affixes, generated in AGR. Tensed verbs, as verbs which have raised to Infl, are available for inflectional affixes, including subject clitic pronouns, to attach to. This analysis of the subject pronoun as syntactic affix is illustrated in (10), using the sentence *il mange* (he eats):

(10)   Proposed S-structure for *il mange*:

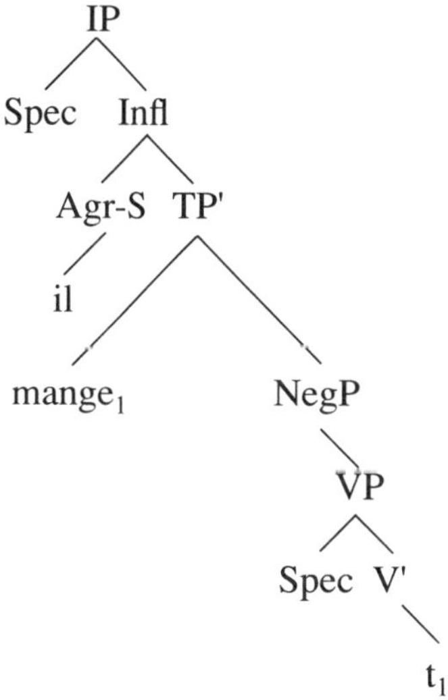

If this analysis of pronominal subjects in French child language is correct, then there should be other ways, apart from the pronoun-tense contingency, to show it. That is, an analysis like that in (10), according to which subject pronouns are syntactically represented as spelling out agreement, predicts that the child's subject pronouns should manifest other distributional properties of syntactic clitics. Further examination of early speech shows, in fact, that they do.

Among the relevant observations is the distinctive positioning of subject pronouns in the word order sequence. Despite the abundance of postverbal subjects in French child language portrayed in chapter 2, subject pronouns never occur in postverbal position. So, while the utterances in (11) are representative of the many pronoun-containing sentences produced by the children,

(11)   Pronominal subjects[5]
    a. il est pas là   e. on marche a l'école (P2–1–3)
       (N2–2–2)   *we walk to school*
      it is not there

    b. et je veux (N2–2–2)   f. elle tombe (P2–2–0)
      and I want   *she falls*

    c. elle dort (D1–8–1)   g. il mange (G1–10–0)
      she sleeps   *he eats*

    d. il veut un bruit   h. je suis là (G2–3–0)
      (D1–11–1)   *I am here*
      he wants a noise

the structures in (12) are exactly those which do not occur. That is, just as there are no subject pronouns in nonfinite clauses (with very few exceptions), there are no subject pronouns in postverbal position:

(12)   Pronominal structures NOT occurring in child language
    [−finite]   [postverbal subject clitics]
    a. il etre pas là   e. et veux je
    b. elle dormir   f. veut il un bruit/veut un bruit il
    c. on marcher a l'école   g. tombe elle
    d. il manger   h. suis je là/suis là je

While I will not explore the acquisition of interrogatives here (see Pierce and Deprez, 1990, for some discussion), it should be noted that the absence of clitics in postverbal positions generalizes to an early but enduring lack of clitic inversion in interrogative environments where it is grammatical and sometimes required.

That children are distinguishing between these clitics pronouns and other pronouns is demonstrated by their use of the common strong form pronoun *moi* (me). Three of the four children (the exception being Nathalie) make widespread use of *moi* in both dislocation and nondislocation constructions. Let's first consider how this pronoun is used when it is not explicitly dislocated, as this usage is more likely to parallel that of clitic pronouns; I will consider the dislocation facts a little later on. First of all, observe in (13) that *moi* is frequently placed in postverbal position:

(13)   a. bois peu moi (D1–8–1)
           drink little me
        b. veux crayon moi (D1–10–2)
           want pencil me
        c. est tombé moi (P2–1–3)
           is fallen me
        d. va voir papa moi (P2–2–0)
           goes to see papa me
        e. moi fais tout seul moi (G2–1–3)
           me do all by myself me
        f. a peur moi (G2–3–0)
           is scared me

In fact, all three children exhibit a preference for postverbal over preverbal position in the placement of *moi*. This contrasts in the obvious way with the positioning of weak form subject pronouns.

More revealing in my view, however, is the occurrence of *moi* in both finite and nonfinite sentences. So, even when *moi* occurs in preverbal position, it is likely to occur in the context of a nonfinite verb. Examples of *moi* in untensed clauses in both pre- and postverbal position are given in (14):

(14)   a. moi pousser (D1–9–3)
           me push$_{-fin}$

   b. moi dessiner la mer (D1–10–2)

   me draw$_{-fin}$ the sea

   c. vider la terre moi (P2–2–0)

   empty$_{-fin}$ the ground me

   d. aller dedans moi (G2–3–0)

   go$_{-fin}$ inside me

   e. toi venir (G2–3–0)

   you go$_{-fin}$

Tests of the relationship between pronoun (weak or strong) and finite status produced highly significant results for each of the children, showing that, while weak subject pronouns distribute only with finite verbs, strong form pronouns distribute in a significantly different manner in that they occur with both finite and nonfinite verbs.[6]

Let's now consider the syntactic behavior of pronouns in so-called dislocation constructions. I will return to the general issue of dislocation, and the relationship between dislocation and other postverbal subjects, in chapter 7. My interest in dislocations here is simply in demonstrating further that French speaking two year-olds are making principled distinctions between clitic and nonclitic pronouns. Just as it is observed that only strong form pronouns occur in postverbal position, so it is observed that only strong form pronouns occur in dislocated positions, whether to the left of a clitic subject or at the end of a sentence. Some examples are shown in (15):

   (15)   a. moi je vais faire café moi (D1–11–1)

           me I go to make coffee me

           b. moi je tousse encore (P2–2–2)

           me I cough again

           c. moi je veux regarder (G2–3–0)

           me I want to watch

Absent are any instances in which the clitic occurs to the left of the nonclitic pronoun (i.e., **je moi* ...), or in postverbal position. By occurring in dislocated positions, *moi* behaves much like a lexical NP. This clearly cannot be said of the clitic subject pronouns.

A final environment I would like to consider is clausal conjunction. Recall that one test of syntactic clitichood of subject pronouns is how they behave under clausal conjunction. Subject clitics in the Northern Italian dialects, it was noted, can not be predicated of a conjunction of verbal clauses. Rather, the clitic is always repeated in both conjuncts, as was illustrated in (7) above. Turning to the French child language data, I encountered suggestive evidence that this generalization also characterizes early French. That is, the available data suggest that repetition of the subject clitic in the second conjunct is obligatory.

It should be noted that this particular discussion is based on a limited amount of data from one of the four children, as there is only extensive enough longitudinal data for this analysis from the child Philippe. I counted 10 instances of clausal conjunction in the Philippe transcripts up to three years, and there were no exceptions to the stated generalization. That is, for Philippe, the conjunction of tensed clauses with a pronominal subject invariably involves repetition of the subject pronoun. At the same time, Philippe commits no errors in which a subject pronoun is separated from the verb, modified, or conjoined to another NP. In (16) are some examples of pronouns in conjoined clauses:

(16) a. Moi je sautes et je descends (P2–2–1)
        Me I jump and I go down

     b. Il se ouvre et il se ferme (P2–3–0)
        It opens and it closes

     c. Je vais ouvrir le couvercule et je vais faire... (P2–9–0)
        I'm going to open the cover and I'm going to...

     d. Ben on ouvre et puis on, on prend le gateau (P2–11–3)
        One opens (it) and then one, one takes the cake

     e. Je le met dedans et puis je le tiens (P3–0–1)
        I put it inside and then I hold it

In addition, Grégoire produced one sentence with clausal conjunction, and it too conforms to the relevant generalization:

(17)   Elle descent et elle remonte sur la main de maman
        (G2–3–0)
        It goes down and it goes back up on mommy's hand

In examples (16b and e), all preverbal clitics recur along with
inflection in the second conjunct. With conjunction of untensed
clauses, as in the case of conjoined past participles, the pronoun, as
expected, does not recur:

(18)   J'ai joué et travaillé (P2–6–3)
        I (have) played and worked

The behavior of subject pronouns in early French conjunction is even
more convincing as evidence for a syntactic clitic analysis when compared to the parallel domain in English, as I discuss below. I have
argued in this section that the distribution of weak subject pronouns in
child French reflects their underlying analysis as inflectional affixes. I
supported this claim by showing that these pronouns (1) always occur
with finite verbs, (2) never occur in postverbal or dislocated position,
and (3) recur as a rule in the second conjunct under the conjunction of
IPs. These observations gain import when they are juxtaposed with
other child languages. I turn now to a comparative survey of subject
pronouns in early English.

5.3 A COMPARATIVE LOOK AT THE ENGLISH DATA

Though some have suggested that subject pronouns in nonstandard
dialects of English are, like subject pronouns in spoken French, in the
process of being demoted to clitic status (see, e.g. Givon, 1976, p.
155; Lightfoot, 1991, p. 170), there are many indications that spoken
French is much further along in this process than English. Generally
speaking, then, there is no reason to expect children acquiring English
to treat subject pronouns as inflectional affixes. And, as I show here,
the data indicate that subject pronouns are not syntactic clitics in
English child language. It is nonetheless intriguing that, by two years
of age, French and English speaking children arrive at such different

analyses of personal subject pronouns. At the same time, the fact that subject pronouns behave one way in early French and another way in early English is, in and of itself, support for the proposed analysis of the French facts.

Recalling the important observation that subject pronouns in early French are contingent upon finite Infl, how can the hypothesis that the same contingency does not hold true for early English be evaluated? Since nonfinite verbs are generally not marked as such by the presence of infinitival *to* at the relevant phase in development, and since inflectional morphology is slow to emerge in English, is there any way to distinguish finite from nonfinite verbs? In recent years, it has often been argued that the latter question should not even be posed. According to Guilfoye and Noonan (1988), Radford (1990) and others, the early grammar lacks Infl altogether, entailing that all verbs produced up to about two years of age are not marked for tense. If this approach is correct, then I need go no further: if all verbs are not finite and children are producing subject pronouns (which they are), then there is no relationship between pronoun occurrence and properties of Infl in early English. However, if the no-Infl approach is seriously flawed, as I claim, then the question of how to distinguish finite from nonfinite forms at the early stage is worth asking.

Let's first consider early utterances which lack appropriate subject-verb agreement, of which there are many. Perhaps not surprisingly, these utterances often contain the subject pronouns *he*, *she* or *it*. Some examples from each of the four children are given in (19):

(19)   a. he sell ice cream (Eve 1–8–0)
        b. it break (Eve 1–6–2)
        c. she drink out a cup (Eve 1–9–2)

        d. it hurt (Naomi 1–10–3)
        e. she like it (Naomi 2–0–3)

        f. he fall down (Nina 1–11–2)
        g. he bite my fingers (Nina 2–0–0)
        h. she have jamas on (Nina 2–2–6)

i. there it go (Peter 2–2–1)

j. she come back (Peter 2–5–3)

These sentences explicitly lack the third person singular -*s* ending, yet they also contain subject pronouns. If subject pronouns required finite Infl, as they were found to in early French, we would expect these constructions to be ruled out by the child's grammar.

It is somewhat misleading to single out the utterances in (19) for lack of inflection. Even utterances with technically correct subject-verb agreement in the present preterite tense often sound awkwardly inflectionless. Although the utterances with first and second singular pronouns in (20) are basically grammatical, they contain correct subject-verb agreement by virtue of the fact that the correct marking is no marking. Since use of the present preterite is strictly limited in English, it is defendable to describe the sentences in (20) as inflectionally bare, as in missing auxiliaries and the participial form of the verb, or missing the past tense -*ed* ending:[7]

(20)　　a. I fall (Eve 1–6–0)

　　　　b. you find it (Eve 1–6–0)

　　　　c. I drop it (Naomi 1–10–2)

　　　　d. you drink (Naomi 2–0–0)

　　　　e. I turn door (Nina 2–0–1)

　　　　f. you like this bug? (Nina 2–0–0)

　　　　g. I do it (Peter 1–11–2)

　　　　h. I get down (Peter 2–0–1)

More obviously missing inflectional material are instances in which the auxiliary is dropped in adjectival and present participle constructions. But these structures, too, often occur with subject pronouns. In (21) are some examples of this prevalent phenomenon:

(21)　　a. I banging (Eve 1–7–2)

　　　　b. he giving hay giraffe (Eve 1–9–0)

    c. I washing (Naomi 1–10–2)

    d. they all sleeping (Naomi 2–1–2)

    e. I popping balloons (Nina 2–0–2)

    f. it hard (Nina 1–11–2)

    g. he walking (Peter 2–1–0)

    h. it dirty (Peter 2–1–3)

These utterances and the many others just like them show that subject pronouns distribute in clauses with missing auxiliary verbs. This is an especially revealing context, since auxiliary verbs raise to Infl and are therefore in a position to bind tense and agreement morphology in Infl. If subject pronouns were agreement affixes in English, we might expect them to be filtered out in the absence of a raised auxiliary.

Summarizing up to this point, I argued that there is no evidence of a contingency between subject pronouns and tensed Infl in English child language, as there was found to be in French child language. In fact, subject pronouns in early English readily occur in explicitly nonfinite clauses. Continuing to compare English and French point for point in this domain, one area of parity concerns the ordering of subject pronouns with respect to verbs. Just as in the child French, I found nominative pronouns are never positioned postverbally in child English. However, this is not of much interest when one considers, recalling chapter 2, that postverbal subjects are generally rare in English child language.

Turning to the next point of comparison, does the distribution of nominative Case pronouns contrast in the relevant manner with that of non-nominative pronouns? In researching this question, I came across numerous utterances in which an accusative pronoun was used in subject position.[8] As shown in (22), these include not only *me*, but also *him* and *her*:

(22)   a. him writing (Eve 1–8–2)

        b. me come back (Eve 1–10–0)

        c. me lay down (Naomi 2–0–0)

        d. does him fish? (Naomi 2–2–0)

>   e. her holding a balloon (Nina 2–0–0)
>   f. him can't see (Naomi 2–2–0)
>
>   g. her too cold (Peter 2–1–0)
>   h. no me take it off (Peter 2–1–3)

Unlike French, therefore, both nominative and accusative pronouns occur in subject position during an early period in English development.[9] The data in (22) is a further indication that nominative Case pronouns in English are not generated in AGR. If they were, we would not observe accusative pronouns occurring in the same environments.

Once again in contrast to the French corpora, I found no evidence of subject dislocation in the English child language data. While the mothers of the four children occasionally produced dislocated subjects in the form of appositives (e.g., *Say "music", Eve; You sit down Pete*), the children themselves did not. The one noteworthy exception that comes to mind was produced by another child, Adam (Brown, 1973), and is shown in (23):

(23)   I Adam don't sit (2–4–3)

While this is only one utterance, it is clearly not the kind of dislocation found in child French. In fact, the subject pronoun itself is dislocated and separated from the negative auxiliary by a name. The only sort of dislocation that is found to be productive in early English involves clitization of the object pronoun *it* alongside the lexical NP object. Examples from each of the four children are presented in (24):

(24)   a. see it paper (Eve 1–7–2)
         b. open it, bouillon cube (Eve 1–8–0)

         c. need it jacket (Naomi 1–10–0)
         d. I want it hug (Naomi 1–10–2)

         e. pat it, rabbit (Nina 1–11–2)
         f. my have it whistle (Nina 2–0–2)

g. close it, dump truck (Peter 1–11–2)

h. can't find it pencil (Peter 2–1–3)

This brings me to the final and most interesting source of comparison to French in this domain, clausal conjunction. The grammar of English allows both repetition and omission of the subject in the second conjunct of a clausal conjunction. That is, both (25a) and (25b) are acceptable, although (25b) has an emphatic reading:

(25)   a. She reads and writes

        b. She reads and she writes

Recall the generalization, based on the Northern Italian dialects, that subject clitics are always repeated under clausal conjunction. (25a) is good in English because subject pronouns are not syntactic clitics. However, it was observed above that subject pronouns strongly tend to be repeated in this context in the speech of French children. What about English speaking children? In contrast to the findings for French, the English data reveal language appropriate non repetition of the subject pronoun.[10]

(26)   a. Put my head down and cough (Eve 1–11–0)

        b. We goed to the beach and saw... (Eve 2–2–0)

        c. We goes to bed and wake up in the morning
           (Eve 2–3–0)

        d. You cut it in little pieces and bite it this way
           (Eve 2–1–0)

        e. Walk in a circle and fall down like me did
           (Peter 2–5–3)

        f. I roll it up and put the band (Peter 2–6–2)

        g. Stepped on a shell and cut you finger (Peter 2–8–2)

        h. They wake up and sleep in that bed (Peter 2–8–2)

        i. You take this off and take that off (Peter 2–3–3)

        j. I up by taking a bath and tell the story about...
           (Naomi 3–5–0)

    k. And you walk around the house and look outside
       (Naomi 3–5–0)
    l. Could I sit down in chair and read the catalogue?
       (Naomi 2–3–0)

    m. I go and pick them up (Nina 2–3–0)
    n. I have my eye and hurt (Nina 2–1–2)
    o. me and all going (Nina 2–1–2)

    p. He puts his instruments and listens to my ear
       (April 2–9–0)[11]
    q. I was falling down the stairs and went boom and hit
       my... (Mark 2–5–0)[12]

At the same time, there are of course examples of conjoined IP's in
which two subjects that are disjoint in reference are pronounced (e.g.
Leila have clay and Nina have clay, Nina 2–1–3; *her hurting and my
fix it*, Nina 2–2–1). There are also numerous grammatical examples of
conjunction of embedded VPs, where repetition of the pronoun would
be ungrammatical:

   (27)   a. I going down and see Fraser (Eve (2–0))
          b. I going go and see Fraser (Eve (2–0))
          c. Hab go doctor and put bandaid on it (Eve (2–1))
          d. I gotta hurry and get some milk (Peter (2–7))
          e. I go put 'em on and skate (Peter (2–7))

Finally, while conjunction of a weak subject pronoun and an NP is
ungrammatical in French (e.g. *Jean et il partiront bientot* (Jean and
he will leave soon)) and unobserved in French child language, I found
examples of the grammatical equivalent in the English child language
data, as in (28):

   (28)   a. You and I have some grape juice (Eve 2–2–0)
          b. Peter and he see Roy (April 2–1–0)

On the basis of the data presented above, then, one can argue that the subject pronoun is not in inflection in the syntax for the English speaking child. For the French child, on the other hand, the analysis of the subject pronoun as a syntactic clitic holds up under the relevant tests. Early French subject pronouns can be distinguished from other NPs, and from subject pronouns in early English, given their inability to be separated from the tensed verb. The relationship between child and adult French in this domain is taken up in chapter 7. This chapter has focused on differing patterns in the first language acquisition of French and English subject pronouns. In it I have amassed evidence for the clitic status of subject pronouns in the syntax of child French on the one hand, and the nonclitic NP status of subject pronouns in the syntax of child English on the other. Let me end by presenting the results of comparing French and English acquisition in terms of the overall proportions of pronominal subjects, by way of leading up to the topic of the next chapter, which is null subjects.

My analysis of subject pronouns in French implies that French is (or is fairly far along on its way to becoming) a null subject language with obligatory subject clitics marking agreement. This analysis leads to a testable prediction concerning subject pronouns in French versus English development. Namely, it is predicted that the speech of French children will contain a progressively greater proportion of subject pronouns than English child language. A difference between English and French in terms of the proportion of sentential utterances which contain subject pronouns is indeed observed. At roughly the 24 to 27 month phase, the four English speaking children average 27% of sentences containing subject pronouns (standard deviation = 4.8). At the same age, the four French speaking children average 46% of sentences containing subject pronouns (standard deviation = 11.1). The two proportions are suggestively different. In fact, by three years of age, Philippe (the only child for whom I have access to substantially older speech samples) is producing 95% of his utterances with subject clitic pronouns.

NOTES

[1] Kayne (1983) abandons this view, claiming instead that French subject pronouns are phonological, but not syntactic, clitics.

[2] All examples in (1) through (5) are from Jaeggli (1982), p. 90–92.

[3] The Trentino examples in (6), (7) and (9) are from Rizzi (1986b). That in (8) is from Brandi and Cordin (1989).

[4] Brandi and Cordin (1989) note that subject clitics in Fiorentino can occur either to the left or the right of the negative clitic.

[5] In the presentation of these examples, as in some other examples which follow, the child is denoted by the first letter of his or her name.

[6] This finding has implications for the analysis of *me* in child English. While it may appear as though children use *me* and *I* interchangeably in early English, more subtle distributional tests may reveal otherwise.

[7] This assumes, based on discourse context, that the second person cases in (20) are nonimperative.

[8] To a lesser extent, there is also use of the genitive form *my* in subject position (e.g. *my take a bath*, Nina 2–1–1) by some children. Unlike the accusative, only the first person singular genitive is used as a subject. Based on this observation, and the fact that the genitive form is never used as a subject by French speaking children, its used by English speaking children may not be of theoretical interest, contrary to Lebeaux (1987). One, albeit uninteresting, possibility is that the *my* used by some English speaking children in subject position is not the genitive, but is rather a phonological blending of *I* and *me*. This would explain why this phenomenon does not generalize to the acquisition of other languages.

[9] In linc with my suggestions as how Case is assigned to the VP-internal subject in child language, this provides evidence that the relevant Case-assigning mechanism is not Spec-Head agreement.

[10] Once again, note that there are few cases, most from older stages. According to Lust (1977; 1980), clausal conjunction becomes productive only at about two and a half years.

[11] April is one of the children studied in Higginson (1985).

[12] Mark is one of the children in MacWhinney and Snow (1985).

CHAPTER 6

NULL SUBJECTS

...as egocentric speech develops it shows a tendency toward an altogether specific form of abbreviation: namely, omitting the subject of a sentence and all words connected with it, while preserving the predicate. This tendency toward predication appears in all our experiments with such regularity that we must assume it to be a basic syntactic form of inner speech. (Vygotsky, 1962, p. 139).

In arguing that very young French and English speaking children have syntactically distinct representations for nominative Case pronouns, the previous chapter demonstrated the use of certain unobvious techniques for evaluating early grammatical knowledge. In considering null subjects in early speech, this chapter also attempts to go beyond the superficial observation that both French and English child language have null subjects. I claim instead that the null subject property of French child language can be distinguished from that of English child language, both in terms of the sources for null subjects and in terms of the behavior of null subjects over the course of development.

The observation that subjects are frequently dropped in early English has long been a focus of research and analysis in the study of child language. The relevant facts have been described from a variety of perspectives, including theories of processing bottlenecks (Pinker, 1984; Bloom, 1989), semantic-pragmatic constraints (Bates, 1976; Greenfield and Smith, 1976), perceptual biases (Brown and Bellugi, 1964; Read and Schreiber, 1982) and Universal Grammar (Hyams, 1986a; Guilfoyle, 1984; Hyams and Jaeggli, 1988). Researchers report maximal frequencies of subject omission at a particular stage, roughly until the age of two and a half years, between 30% (cf. Valian, 1989) and 65% (cf. Hyams and Jaeggali (1988), based on the Brown corpus for the child Adam). Importantly, it has been found that, while subjects are omitted from roughly half of all verb containing utterances at an early stage in English acquisition, objects are usually not omitted. According to Bloom (1989), who reports an average of 55% subject deletion across three children at this stage, objects are omitted from obligatory contexts only 9% of the time.

I contend here that subject deletion in the early stages of English and French child languages follows from the VP-internal subject configuration, just as it does in adult languages with VP-internal subjects. Given the mechanism of Case assignment in early child language as outlined above (in chapter 1), the VP-internal subject position is assigned structural nominative Case. Since the licensing of *pro* subjects is coextensive with the domain of nominative Case assignment, as Rizzi (1986a), Koopman and Sportiche (1988) and others have claimed, then it follows that *pro* is licensed in VP-internal subject position. I further assume, following Jaeggli and Hyams (1988), that *pro* is identified by an empty discourse topic (cf. Huang, 1984) in early English and French child language, given the absence of overt specification of agreement at this stage.[1]

It is traditionally held that the adult grammars of English and French are equivalent in their failure to license null subjects. By adopting the view, following Jaeggli (1982) and others, that subject pronouns in French are syntactic clitics, I am also maintaining that French is a null subject language. If the two adult grammars are not alike in this respect, then there is reason to expect differences in the child grammars along the same lines. Specifically, it is predicted that the null subject property of English will disappear at a fairly young age, while the null subject property of French will endure. Given the role of subject clitics in French as markers of agreement, it also follows that there are in effect two sources for apparent null subjects in early French: the (largely ungrammatical) absence of overt agreement and the (grammatical) occurrence of a null VP-internal subject. Therefore, in quantifying empty subjects in early French, utterances with overt agreement but no lexical subject should also be counted as null subject sentences. I turn first to null subjects in French child language and show how the two sources of apparent null subjects can be distinguished.

6.1 NULL SUBJECTS IN FRENCH CHILD LANGUAGE

In the data I have examined, a large percentage of child utterances lack both a grammatical subject and a subject clitic. Such utterances contain either finite or nonfinite verbs, as illustrated in (1):

(1)   *finite*

    a. est pas gros (N2–2–2)
       (*is not big*)

    b. va chercher l'auto (N2–2–2)
       (*goes to look for the car*)

    c. avant veux chocolat (P2–2–0)
       (*before want chocolate*)

    d. est cassé (P2 1–3)
       (*is broken*)

    e. boit (D1–9–3)
       (*drinks*)

    f. veut lait (D1–11–1)
       (*wants milk*)

    g. est tombé (G1–10–3)
       (*is fallen*)

    h. veux monter (G1–10–0)
       (*want to climb*)

  nonfinite

    i. pas manger (N1–10–2)
      (*not eat*)

    j. tomber (N1–9–30)
      (*fall*)

    k. lancer la balle (P2–1–3)
      (*throw the ball*)

    l. chercher les crayons (P2–2–1)
      (*look for the crayons*)

    m. enlever papier (D1–9–3)
      (*lift paper*)

    n. dormir tout nu (D1–10–2)
      (*sleep all naked*)

    o. ouvrir (G1–9–2)
      (*open*)

    p. regarder Adrien (G1–11–3)
      (*watch Adrien*)

The absence of subject clitics in the nonfinite sentences of the right column is exactly as expected, given, as I have just shown, that subject clitics in French child language never occur with nonfinite verbs. The lack of subject clitics in finite sentences, however, is not so easily explained. Although it may indicate that subject agreement marking is optional in the child's grammar, I think it is more likely the result of certain output limitations and of gradual acquisition of these morphemes. Although I will not spell out an analysis along these lines here, I describe a gradual rise of subject clitics to near obligatory status below.

I take the fact that null subjects occur in both finite and nonfinite clauses as proof that they are not simply missing subject clitics. If they are not missing subject clitics, then they are true empty subjects, presumably located in VP-internal position. A glance at the actual distributions of null subjects over finite and nonfinite clauses, in comparison to that of pronominal subjects, is helpful in illustrating this point:

(2)

	finite	*nonfinite*
Daniel		
pronominal subjects	104	14
null subjects	247	273
Grégoire		
pronominal subjects	143	3
null subjects	158	108
Nathalie		
pronominal subjects	162	7
null subjects	90	131
Philippe		
pronominal subjects	196	3
null subjects	90	34

While pronominal subjects almost never occur in nonfinite clauses, null subjects distribute fairly equally between finite and nonfinite clauses.

Another important point about null subjects in French child lan-

guage is that, although there is an overall decrease, they do not appear
to be going away. In the oldest transcripts I considered for each child
(i.e. Daniel at 1–11–1, Grégoire at 2–3–0, Nathalie at 2–3–2, and
Philippe at 2–3–0), the proportion of utterances with null subjects
was still quite high, ranging from 35 to 52%. As you will see shortly,
this contrasts with the early drop off in the rate of null subjects
observed in English child language. Given the adopted analysis of
pronominal subjects, it is in fact misleading to take into account only
sentences like those in calculating the rate of subject omission.
Because subject clitics are generated in Infl, they do not count as
grammatical subjects. Therefore, the correct way to count null subjects
includes both sentences like those in (1) and all sentences with a
pronominal subject and no lexical subject. Consider the six variations
on a single sentence that may be found in French child language, as
portrayed in (3) (details aside):

(3)   a. parle (*speaks*)

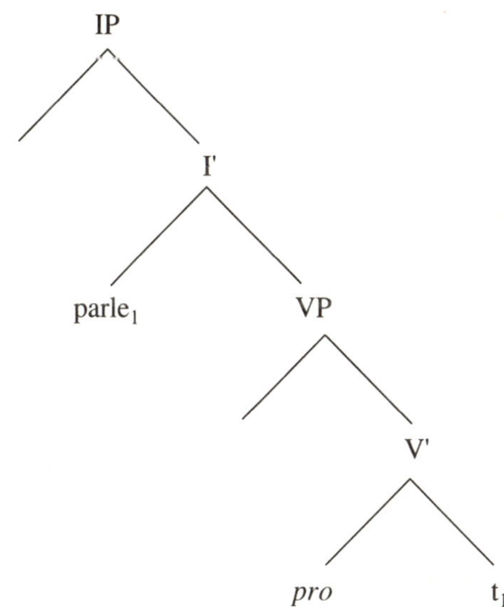

b. parle Marie (*speaks Marie*)

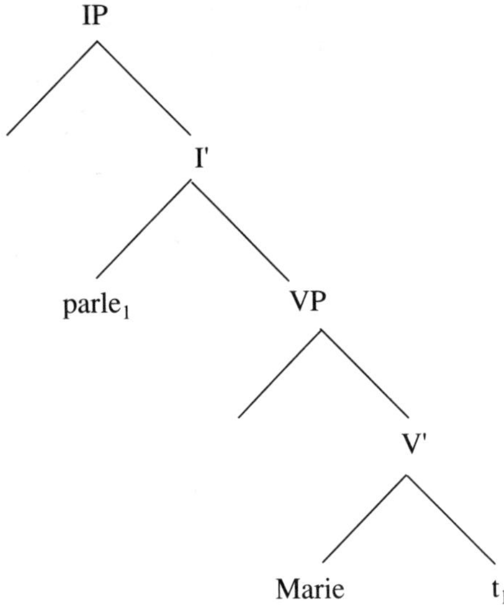

c. elle parle (*she-speaks*)

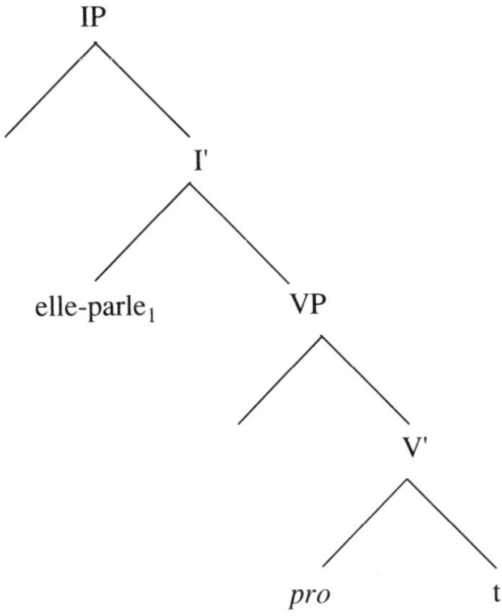

d. elle parle Marie (*she-speaks Marie*)

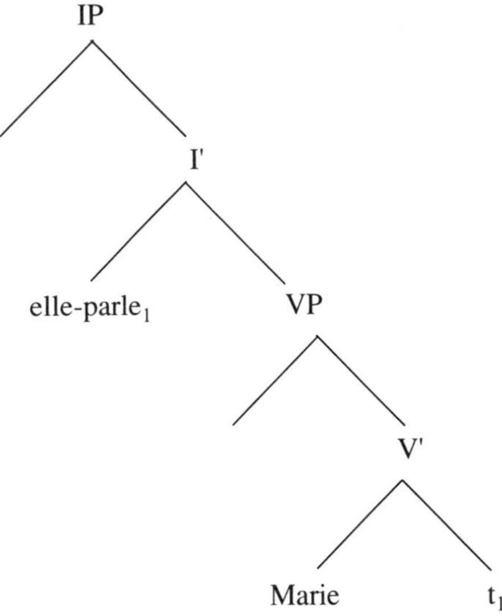

e. Marie parle (*marie speaks*)

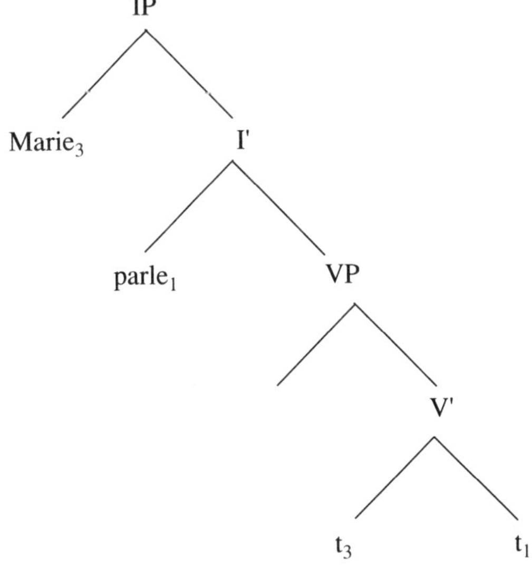

f. Marie elle parle (*Marie she-speaks*)[2]

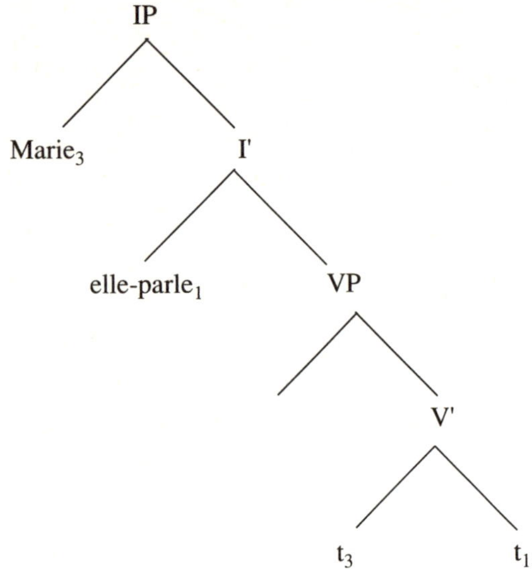

(3a) and (3b) lack the overt clitic marker of agreement and are ungrammatical in the adult language. (3a), but not (3b), also contains a null subject. (3c) is the null subject construction that is accepted by the adult grammar. (3d) and (3f) are dislocation constructions found in both the child language and the adult language, while (3e), the simple subject-verb construction, is rather rare in both child and adult languages (Francois, 1974).

If (3c) is included in the count of null subjects, as the theory requires, then a surprising result emerges: the rate of null subjects over the course of development during this early period remains constant, and at fairly high rate, for all four children. The actual percentages are listed in (4):[3]

(4)

Grégoire

G1   (1–9–2)   57%
G2   (1–10–0)   47%

G3	(1–10–3)	56%
G4	(1–11–3)	68%
G5	(2–0–1)	69%
G6	(2–1–3)	72%
G7	(2–3–0)	62%

Nathalie

N1	(1–9–3)	47%
N2	(1–10–1)	53%
N4	(2–0–1)	65%
N6	(2–2–2)	61%
N7	(2–3–2)	88%

Daniel

D1	(1–8–1)	87%
D2	(1–8–3)	82%
D3	(1–9–3)	90%
D4	(1–10–2)	77%
D5	(1–11–1)	79%

Philippe

P1	(2–1–3)	70%
P2	(2–2–0)	79%
P3	(2–2–1)	63%
P4	(2–2–2)	65%
P7	(2–3–0)	79%

If only constructions of the (3a) type are included in this calculation, the percentages drop substantially over time, rather than remaining constant. Null subject sentences with missing subject clitics account for 40% (versus 62%) of Grégoire's utterances at 2–3–0, 27% (versus 88%) of Nathalie's utterances at 2–3–2, 56% (versus 79%) of Daniel's utterances at 1–11–1 and 49% (versus 79%) of Philippe's utterances at 2–3–0.

I have presented these figures because they will prove useful in comparing the behavior of null subjects in French acquisition to that in English acquisition. Before turning to the English data, it is worth mentioning that there is evidence that null subjects and subject clitics in French develop along the lines expected by the model. In the speech of the one child for whom I have examined older longitudinal data

(Philippe), it is indeed observed that null subjects of the type in (1) and (3a) completely disappear by 32 months of age, by which time pronominal subjects are occurring in 95% of all sentential utterances.

6.2 A COMPARATIVE LOOK AT ENGLISH ACQUISITION

From the hypothesis that the early child grammar of English licenses VP-internal subjects at S-structure, it follows that English child sentences will contain both unraised VP-internal subjects, and null subjects. Previous chapters in this book have been devoted to substantiating the claim that early English is characterized by unraised VP-internal subjects. Such subjects are directly observable in the context of negation and auxiliary verbs. Utterances which contain overt subjects but which lack clues as to the structural position of those subjects are also assumed, by deduction, to be situated within the VP during the relevant developmental period.[4] The claim that English child language has null subjects is readily substantiated, as I now discuss. A final section of this chapter deals directly with the proposed account of these empty subjects.

In the youngest portion of the English data I have analyzed, null subject sentences account for 45 to 90% of all verb containing utterances. (5) through (8) contain only a few of the hundreds of null subject sentences recorded for each of four children.

(5)   *Naomi*
        a. bang foot (1–10–1)   e. can make tail (1–11–3)
        b. playing ball (1–10–1)   f. changing (1–11–0)
        c. find Georgie (1–11–0)   g. want more (1–10–2)
        d. is broken (1–11–3)   h. get clip (1–11–0)

(6)   *Peter*
        a. found it (1–11–2)   e. get down, I get down
        b. need it (1–11–2)   (2–1–0)
        c. broke this (2–0–1)   f. goes right here (2–1–0)
        d. goes front (2–0–1)   g. fall down (2–1–3)
                                       h. fit like that (2–1–3)

(7)   *Nina*
       a. climbing leaf (1–11–1)   e. feed the lama (2–0–0)
       b. pat kitty cat (1–11–1)   f. hug a monkey (2–0–0)
       c. hurt (1–11–3)   g. riding my bicycle (2–0–1)
       d. fall down (1–11–3)   h. drinking milk (2–0–1)

(8)   *Eve*
       a. drop nut (1–7–2)   e. going bye-bye (1–8–2)
       b. lying down (1–7–2)   f. wipe finger (1–8–2)
       c. want find top (1–8–0)   g. forgot bibby (1–9–0)
       d. came back (1–8–0)   h. eating popcorn (1–9–0)

In each case where it was not possible to determine whether an utterance was nonimperative on the basis of its form, discourse context was appealed to; verbs in past tense form (e.g. (8g)) or progressive participle form (e.g. (7h)) are transparently nonimperative. I assume that *pro* in this early construction is licensed by directional (i.e. rightward) Infl-government in a structure such as (9):

(9)

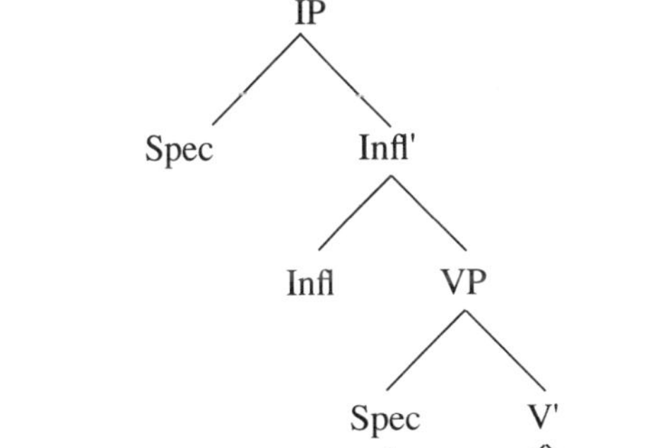

It is interesting to note that there was no significant difference between bare stem verbs and progressive participles in terms of the proportion of null versus overt subjects that they distribute with. Chi-square tests of contingency produced nonsignificant results in the case of three out of four children, measured individually. This fact serves to challenge the view that null subjects in English child language result from output limitations alone. If the number of morphemes in the VP was the sole predictor of when a subject would be dropped, we would expect to find a greater rate of subject omission in the context of verbs of the forms *V +ing* than in the context of verbs of bare stem form.[5]

Returning to the main concern here, that of comparing French and English child language, I turn now to developmental changes in the rate of subject omission. As exhibited above in (4), the rate of subject omission in French does not appear to decrease over the course of acquisition. The same cannot be said of English acquisition. A glance at the changing percentages of null subject utterances reveals a rapid decline:

(10)   *Nina*
         age 1–11–2:   44% null subjects (out of all utterances)
         age 2–2–0:   11% null subjects

         Peter
         age 1–11–2:   90% null subjects
         age 2–3–3:   16% null subjects

         Naomi
         age 1–10–1:   47% null subjects
         age 2–1–3:   6% null subjects

         Eve
         age 1–7–2:   57% null subjects
         age 1–11–2:   8% null subjects

As another way of characterizing the relationship between the decline in null subjects and age, (11) lists the approximate ages at which each of the four children reached a level of 15% null subjects out of all utterances:

(11)   Nina: 2–2–0
          Peter: 2–3–3
          Naomi: 2–0–1
          Eve: 1–11–2

Although Eve is clearly developing more rapidly than the other three children, it can safely be said that children acquiring English generally emerge out of the null subject between two and two and a half years. This contrasts in an obvious manner with the findings for French acquisition, where the rate of subject omission does not decline at all.

The percentages in (10) reflect the total number of verb containing utterances that are produced without an overt subject. Under the hypothesis that null subjects are VP-internal subjects, these percentages also reflect the proportion of VP-internal subjects. But the question arises as to how one can determine that a given overt subject is a VP-internal or VP-external subject in child language. That is, given that overt subjects which can only be analyzed as VP-internal subjects are observed, namely those that occur to the right of negation and auxiliaries, it may well be that other overt subjects produced during the period of frequent subject omission are also VP-internal subjects.

A more detailed examination of null subject environments suggests that this is indeed the case. Specifically, the rate of subject omission in the context of noncontracted auxiliary verbs does not decline as rapidly as the overall rate.[6] At an intermediate period of overall subject drop for Nina, between 2–1–1 and 2–1–3 when her overall proportion of null subject sentences is 27%, the proportion of noncontracted auxiliaries preceded by a null subject is 85%. Furthermore, when her overall rate of subject omission reaches 11%, the rate with auxiliaries remains fairly high, at 49%. Looking at Peter, at the transitional phase in null subjects when the overall rate is 44% (from 2–1– 0 to 2–1–3), the rate with auxiliaries only is 100%. And when the overall rate is at 16%, the rate with auxiliaries is 50%. For Naomi, when the overall pro-drop rate is 50% (from 1–11–2 through 2–0–1), the pro-drop rate with auxiliaries is still 94%; when the overall rate is 6%, the auxiliary pro-drop rate is 50%. Finally, during Eve's intermediate null subject phase (1–10–0) at which point the overall rate of subject omission is 31%, omission of the subject in the context of an auxiliary occurs 77% of the time. When the overall rate is 8%, the rate with auxiliaries is 38%.

According to the model of the grammar I have assumed, this difference in proportion, with the extent of overt subject use in the context of auxiliary verbs remaining depressed, suggests that obligatory subject raising to [Spec, IP] position is slow to be acquired. This implies that overt subjects occurring in the context of main verbs during an early period are likely to be VP-internal. I develop this argument further in the next chapter, comparing the young child's grammar for English to the adult grammar, and calling into question the view that overt subjects in the basic sentences of adult English are necessarily VP-external.

6.3 NULL SUBJECTS OVER THE COURSE OF ACQUISITION

At this point, it would be best to review certain theoretical assumptions and predictions, and evaluate their fit to the acquisition results. Recall that null subjects are explained in the current framework as resulting from the VP-internal subject configuration. According to Sportiche (1988) and Koopman and Sportiche (1988), a *pro* subject is licensed in VP-internal position because Infl head-governs the VP and its specifier. Similarly, according to Adams (1987), null subjects are licensed when they are canonically governed and identified by Infl. Null subjects in child language, therefore, as in adult language, are VP-internal subjects. However, null thematic subjects in child language do not seem to be identified by a rich or strong inflection (Rizzi, 1982). I suggest that identification by discourse topic, along the lines suggested by Huang (1989) for Chinese, operates in early grammar.

In accounting for the fact that empty and overt subjects seem to be licensed in the early language in the environment of tenseless Infl, one can appeal to the argument that an Infl which is empty of phonological features also governs and assigns Case to the subject position.

According to Huang (1989), for example, in providing a government-based account of null subjects and nominative case assignment in Chinese, the finiteness of a clause may be determined in terms of the potential occurrence of overt tensed Infl. In clauses which are potentially finite but which contain a zero-morpheme in Infl, Infl still governs and assigns nominative Case to the lexical subject, and licenses *pro* in subject position. One implication of this account of French child language is that the null subject property we see in the child language does not go away in the adult language. The subject clitics in Infl in the child's grammar are also in Infl in the adult grammar. What presumably does change, however, are the conditions under which *pro* is identified. While *pro* is identified by a discourse topic in child grammar, as Jaeggli and Hyams (1988) have proposed, I suggest that it is identified by overt agreement (that is, by a subject clitic in Agr) in the adult grammar.

Turning to English, consider the range of developmental facts discussed so far from the perspective of timing. In particular, compare the ages in (11) repeated below, the point for each child when the rate of null subjects falls below 15%, with the initial ages at which overt subjects to the left of the negative marker are strongly in evidence, repeated from chapter 3:

(11) Nina: 2–2–0   (12) Nina: 2–1–3
      Peter: 2–3–3   Peter: 2–3–0
      Naomi: 2–0 –1   Naomi: 2–0–1
      Eve: 1–11–2   Eve: 1–11–0

This is an admittedly rough measure, and the match is not precise in all four cases. Yet there is a suggestive closeness in time between the loss of null subjects and the rise of subject movement to [Spec, IP]. Of course, the 18 to 30 month period encompasses so much in terms of grammatical development that one could counter that no overlap of this type is surprising.

As to the question of what would finally exclude the licensing of VP-internal subjects, including null subjects in VP-internal position, my tentative answer is the acquisition of affix-lowering. As mentioned in chapter 4, English speaking children are known to acquire the use of most verbal inflections relatively late. Under the derivational economy approach described there, affix-lowering is expected to be disfavored as a language-specific rule involving more than one derivational step. Assuming, in line with Chomsky (1988), that affix-lowering is a marked parametric option, then this would explain why its acquisition is in fact delayed. Inflectional material that fails to be lowered into VP during an early stage in English acquisition may play a role in licensing VP-internal subjects. Once affix lowering is acquired, the conditions under which VP-internal subjects are licensed would then be voided (assuming that the trace of the lowered agreement affix erases or is otherwise unable to license and/or identify a null subject). Infl which lowers into the VP is not the head of the V-I complex and thus fails to govern the VP-internal subject position. Subject raising to [Spec, IP] for Case reasons becomes necessary. Since there is no affix-lowering in French, overt and null VP-internal subjects continue to be licensed at S-structure. That is, verb raising to Infl in Romance does not void structural assignment of nominative case as Infl is the head of the V-I complex formed by verb raising. Since verb raising voids VP-barrierhood, Infl can assign nominative Case into the VP (Chomsky, 1986b). Note further that the observed tendency towards retention of null subjects in sentences with auxiliaries is exactly as expected given this explanation for the loss of null subjects in English development. Infl does not lower when an auxiliary or modal is generated, so the structural conditions under which null subjects are licensed are not affected.

Summarizing, I have tried to show how the null subject property of early French can be distinguished from that of early English, in terms of the sources of null subjects as well as the extent of subject omission over the course of development. While null subjects in French were found to endure, null subjects in English decline to a minimum at a very early age. This brings me to the topic of the next chapter, the relationship between language acquisition and language change. The claim that French is a null subject language is not uncontroversial. Yet

I have analyzed data from French child language as supporting this view. I now go one step further, in proposing that the clitic status of subject pronouns in spoken French, in interaction with the colloquial variability in word order, is what leads the French language learner to assume that postverbal subjects are licit in the target grammar.

NOTES

[1] That the child at this stage has topicalization is evident from other cases of early A'-movement, such as the well-known early acquisition of wh-movement.

[2] This particular representation is questionable, since the presence of an overt subject clitic in Infl may block government of [Spec, IP] position (cf. Jaeggli, 1982). The left dislocated NP would then be located in topic position.

[3] These percentages are derived as the number of all sentences of type (3a) and (3c) divided by the total number of verb containing utterances in a given transcript.

[4] Recall that, in a similar vein, Contreras (1987) argues that adult English, given affix lowering and assignment of nominative Case under Infl-government to the VP-internal subject, is not a subject raising language.

[5] Although it could be argued, as in chapter 4, that the progressive is a base-generated verbal form, it is nonetheless morphologically complex.

[6] The calculation of percentage of auxiliaries preceded by a null subject takes into consideration only unrehearsed forms. Excluded from the count are constructions that are clearly formulaic for a given child. For example, in Peter's case, sentences beginning with *This is* ... are not included in the count.

CHAPTER 7

LANGUAGE CHANGE

In this chapter, I take a broader perspective on the language acquisition process. While chapters 2 through 6 focused on the early French and English grammars of word order, negation, inflection, pronouns and null subjects, this chapter considers how developmental change comes about in those domains where the grammar appears to undergo change. It also discusses the relationship between acquisition and diachronic change. I have tried to show how child grammars for English and French may be instructively compared, and generally how a comparative approach to child language – even when the focus of comparison is two languages with considerable overlap in syntactic make-up – provides a more detailed look at the structures involved than does examination of one child language alone. As it turns out, English and French also present an interesting opportunity for comparison in terms of diachronic processes. And I would like to argue (perhaps not so originally) that findings in acquisition can provide answers to some of the questions that arise in the study of language change.

7.1 CHANGE AND ACQUISITION IN FRENCH

By way of attempting to answer the question of what leads the child acquiring French to produce postverbal subjects in abundance and to treat subject pronouns as syntactic critics, I give a brief review here of related constructions in adult French speech as discussed in the linguistic literature. The description of subject clitics and inverted word order from a typological perspective, it appears, best captures these phenomena in French child language, and also goes some of the way toward explaining the role of acquisition in language change.

Many linguists working on spoken French have taken the approach that agreement and pronominalization should not be analyzed as distinct processes. Diachronic studies have indeed shown that pronominal elements undergo a natural process of phonological attrition due to their lack of stress. And the cliticization of subject pronouns is thought to be a motivating factor in the fundamental syntactic reanalysis that took place between Old French and Middle French, when French lost the property of being verb-second (cf. e.g. Adams, 1987; Kroch, 1989). But others have taken this view one step further, arguing that cliticized subject pronouns in the spoken version of Modern French have become, or are becoming, obligatory subject agreement markers over the course of language change (Givon, 1976; Harris, 1978; Larsson, 1979; Lambrecht, 1981; Bailard, 1982; Barnes, 1985, among others). Harris (1978), for one, argues that the downgrading of clitic pronouns in French to affixes on the verb is the symptom of a major typological shift in which French is becoming an essentially verb-initial language.[1]

The purported demotion of subject pronouns in French to inflectional prefixes has the effect that, at least in the spoken language, these clitics behave in certain respects like subject clitics in the Northern Italian dialects, discussed briefly in chapter 5.[2] For one, clausal conjunction in spoken French generally involves the repetition of the subject pronoun. According to Lambrecht (1981), the (a) examples in (1) and (2) below are acceptable in written French, but the (b) examples are much more likely to be generated in speech:[3]

(1)   a. Il mange et boit comme un cochon
          (*He eats and drinks like a pig*)
       b. I-mange et i-boit comme un cochon
          (*He eats and he drinks like a pig*)

(2)   a. ?Je lis et puis écris
          (*I read and then write*)
       b. J-lis et puis j-écris
          (*I read and then I write*)

As is clear from the English glosses in each case, (a) and (b) are equally acceptable in English; repetition of the pronouns, as in the (b) examples, simply adds emphasis. Note that the contrast between standard and nonstandard French does not maintain in cases of nonclausal conjunction, such as conjoined participial and infinitival phrases. In these structures, the locus of conjunction is below inflection. If whole clauses of these types are conjoined, either both the auxiliary and the pronoun are repeated or neither are:

(3)   a. Elle a mangé et dansé
           (*She ate and dansed*)
        b. Elle a mangé et elle a dansé
        c. *Elle a mangé et a dansé

In examining the child language data, we encountered clear evidence that Lambrecht's (1981) characterization of spoken French accounts for the French child's clausal conjunction, and that this contrasts with the English child's usage.

Another outcome of subject pronouns being analyzed as agreement prefixes is that they co-occur with other subject NPs. According to Lambrecht (1981), Barnes (1985) and others — and also readily confirmed by anyone who converses in French — sentences containing both a subject clitic and a co-referring NP or emphatic pronoun to its left or right occur quite frequently in spoken French. Left dislocations of the subject, as in (4), were found by Ashby (1988), in a broad study of spoken French, to be somewhat more robust that right dislocations:[4]

(4)   a. Moi je bois énormément
           Me I drink enormous quantities
        b. Ta soupe, elle arrive rose.
           Your (fem.) soup, it (fem.) arrives pink

Many linguists who have analyzed the distribution of left and right dislocations maintain that left dislocation is an essentially pragmatic phenomenon, in that the left-dislocated element usually represents a discourse topic or is being emphasized. In contrast to left dislocations, which tend to be pragmatically and prosodically marked, right dislocations are described as being unmarked in the relevant sense. According to Ashby (1988), right dislocations are generally found not to be pragmatically motivated. Larsson (1979) and Lambrecht (1981) also claim that right dislocated elements do not in general serve a contrastive or emphatic function, and, more importantly, that they tend to be prosodically incorporated into the rest of the sentence. Both of these authors describe them as having flat or equal intonation, a finding which is confirmed by Ashby (1988). In (5) are two examples of transcribed adult right dislocations:[5]

> (5)   a. Il est bien petit ce collier
>   *It$_i$ is pretty small this necklace$_i$*
>   b. Ils vont pas rentrer les autres
>   *They$_i$ won't go back the others$_i$*

Finally, in addition to the conjunction and dislocation facts, as well as the established facts showing the weakness of subject pronouns in French portrayed in (1) through (5) of chapter 5, another parallel between spoken French and Northern Italian dialects with subject critics is the near absence of simple NP subject-VP constructions like *Jean mange* (John eats). Many linguists who have studied the colloquial language concur that this basic form is becoming strikingly rare (cf. Francois, 1974; Lambrecht, 1981). This finding is indeed echoed in the child language data, where I observed a very small number of utterances containing preverbal lexical subjects.

Because it is exactly the spoken language that the child receives as input during the first few years of life, these observations about spoken French cannot be ignored in the study French acquisition. In particular, what is the French child to make of right dislocations in the input if they lack pragmatic and prosodic marking? Without such marking, there is in effect no indication to the child to treat these structures as peripheral exceptions to core conditions on word order. If this is true, it would not be surprising to find that the child's own grammar accommodates these structures. On the basis of natural production data from French child language, I argued earlier that this is indeed the case. There is strong evidence both that subject clitics are in nonargument position in French child language and that postverbal subjects are formally accommodated (i.e. generated) by the French child's grammar. The fact that the child's grammar accommodates these structures may itself be a force in the direction of change in French grammar that many linguists have remarked upon. But before I pursue this line of argumentation further, it would be useful to examine the actual input to the four children whose speech I have been analyzing.

There are many aspects of input speech that potentially relate to language learner's grammatical hypotheses concerning subject clitics and word order.[6] I will only consider three that seem particularly relevant here. One is the proportion and distribution of pronominal subjects. Another is the rate of subject dislocation. And the third is the occurrence of preverbal lexical subjects in the absence of a co-referring subject clitic. In all three respects, as it turns out, the four mothers behave very much like the French speakers portrayed in the preceding paragraphs.[7] The table in (6) presents the basic results of this input survey:

(6)   Aspects of maternal speech

	PHILIPPE	DANIEL	NATHALIE	GREGOIRE
% pronominal subjects	88%	83%	85%	84%
% right dislocation	11%	11%	7%	8%
% left dislocation	2%	4%	10%	9%
% preverbal NP subjects	1%	8%	8%	3%

The four mothers exhibit noteworthy similarity when it comes to the proportion of their sentential utterances which contain a (nonemphatic) pronominal subject. This percentage ranges from 83 to 88% percent depending upon the mother. Pronominal subject utterances include instances of the characteristic repetition of the subject pronoun under clausal conjunction. (7) contains some examples from Philippe's mother, who produced the greatest number of these. (8) contains examples from the other three mothers.

(7)   a. Si tu as froid aux pieds et si tu enleves tes chaussons ...
          (*If you have cold feet and if you take off your slippers ...*)
       b. Tu t'assieds et tu le regardes
          (*You sit down and you watch it*)
       c. Je me l'ai demandé et je l'ai pas trouvé
          (*I asked myself that and I didn't find it*)
       d. Marc il boit et puis il trempe ses trucs
          (*Marc he drinks and then he wets his things*)

(8)   a. Tu prends ceux-la et tu essaies de les mettre (Nathalie's mother)
          (*You take those and you try to put them ...*)
       b. ... on va le casser et après ca on peut plus allumer (Daniel's mother)
          (... *we are going to break it and after that we won't ...*)
       c. Il se precipite et il dit "kiki" (Grégoire's mother)
          (*He throws himself and he says "kiki"*)

Some of these subject pronouns are occurring in left and right dislocations of the subject. Observe in (6) that the percentage of right dislocations (calculated as the number of right dislocations out of all sample utterances) is higher for two of the mothers than that of left dislocations, conflicting with Ashby's (1988) finding that left dislocations outnumber right dislocations in spoken French. But the sample of mothers and of utterances here is clearly too limited to draw any general conclusions. Examples of maternal right dislocations, which accounted for 7 to 11% utterances, are given in (9):

(9)   Maternal right dislocations

       Mother of Nathalie
       (a) Elle va avoir froid la poupée.
           (*She'll be cold the doll*)

(b) Oui, elle fait dodo, la poupée.
     (*Yes, she goes to sleep, the doll*)

Mother of Philippe
(c) Ca saute pas les bateaux
     (*That doesn't jump boats*)
(d) Il est gros ce petit ventre.
     (*It is big this little belly*)

Mother of Grégoire
(e) Il est tombé le morceau
     (*It fell the piece*)
(f) Il a des yeux terrible, ce lion
     (*He has terrible eyes, this lion*)

Mother of Daniel
(g) Elle rit, la petite fille quand il passe, le garçon.
     (*She laughs, the little girl when the passes, the boy*)
(h) Elle a trouvé son couvercle la petite boite.
     (*She found her cover the little box*)

The number of left dislocations produced by mothers was found to be more variable than that of right dislocations, with a range of 2 to 10%. Some examples of these are presented in (10):

(10)   Maternal left dislocations
         a. Toi tu prend la tête de l'éléphant (Grégoire's mother)
            (*You you take the head of the elephant*)
         b. La serviette, elle est blanche, avec un petit dessin
            (Philippe's mother)
            (*The towel, it is white, with a little design . . .*)
         c. Moi j'aime pas (Daniel's mother)
            (*Me I don't like*)
         d. Marc il fait dodo (Nathalie's mother)
            (*Marc he is sleeping*)

Note from (6) that subject dislocation constructions outnumber nondislocated subjects from 13:1 to 2:1 depending upon the mother. While two of the mothers (Philippe's mother and Grégoire's mother) produced very few simple subject sentences, the remaining two mothers produced a substantial 8%. Since there is some variability among mothers, the question naturally arises as to whether these measures of maternal speech produce any correlates in child speech. In a correlation matrix comparing the maternal measures in (6) with matched measures of child speech (based on all available speech samples up to 27 months and therefore averaged across development), the only significant correlation to emerge was that between the proportion of nondislocated lexical subjects in maternal speech and the proportion of postverbal subjects in child speech. Namely, the extent to which mothers produced nondislocated subjects correlates negatively ($r = -0.962$) with the extent to which children produce lexical subjects in postverbal position (with and without subject critics) at a significant level, even with this small sample size ($p. < 0.025$). As this is the outcome of a cursory analysis, and one based on only four mother-child pairs, this result should be regarded as preliminary. How spoken French and French acquisition relate is an area ripe for further careful research.

With this preface, let me continue to interpret this surprising outcome and other results of this survey. In the correlation matrix, the extent to which mothers produce right dislocations was found not to correlate significantly with the child's rate of postverbal subject production. There are, however, other sources of inversion in French speech, including causatives and stylistic inversion in interrogatives. Although these structures occur in the parental speech I examined, they are scarce. Lightbown (1977) also notes that French speaking mothers tend to avoid licensed inversion in yes/no questions and wh-questions, relying instead on intonation to mark questionhood.[8] Thus, it may be concluded, based on the acquisition data for word order described in chapter 2, that the children are producing postverbal subjects far beyond the rate of dislocated postverbal subjects in their linguistic environment. The fact that nondislocated subjects in input correlate negatively with postverbal subjects in the child output is interpretable as showing that children are nonetheless attentive to the extent of explicit subject raising in their linguistic environment. The children whose mothers produced almost no simple subject sentences were more likely to produce unraised VP-internal subjects.

It would be premature at this time to go beyond impressionistic conclusions. Yet these observations can be said to enhance the plausibility of a model which juxtaposes diachronic and acquisitional trends. I return now to the French acquisition data and construct such a model. Specifically, I address the question posed by typologists as to why right dislocated order in French has progressed from being a marked option to being "grammaticalized". By definition, the answer to this question lies in the acquisition process; language change takes place when the child constructs a grammar different from that of the parents (Lightfoot, 1988).

Recall from chapter two that the overwhelming majority of lexical subjects produced by young French-speaking children occur in postverbal position. For the four children whose speech I analyzed, 70% of all lexical subjects in noninterrogatives were positioned postverbally. Sentences with postverbal subjects account for 20% (516/2586) of all verb-containing utterances produced by the children during this relatively early period. Given, as we have just seen, that postverbal subjects in the form of right dislocations in adult speech are neither very frequent nor very salient according to standard measures, what could lead the child to produce them in such quantity and how are they represented in the child's grammar?

It seems plausible that the very lack of pragmatic and prosodic marking on right dislocation constructions contributes to their frequency in child speech. Right dislocated phrases, unlike left dislocated ones, do not play the role of topics. Furthermore, right dislocations do not appear to involve marked stress on the dislocated phrase, or a marked intonational break between that phrase and the rest of the sentence (Larsson, 1979; Lambrecht, 1981). In other words, there does not seem to be any reliable indication to the child, in the form of pragmatic or prosodic cues, that this type of input should be ignored in selecting a grammar. Presumably then, in the absence of any signal to the child to set these structures aside, so to speak, they are incorporated into the developing grammar. In addition, given the relatively low frequency of right dislocations and inversion in the adult spoken language, there is reason to believe that inherent grammatical factors, and not just input factors, play a key rule in the child's production of postverbal subjects. Among these inherent grammatical factors are the raising of the verb to Infl and the generation of the subject within the VP.

The answer to the typologists' question now seems rather obvious. The child can't help but to reanalyze right dislocations in a grammaticalized fashion, because the child has no way of knowing that they are not grammatical in input and, more importantly, because they confirm the child's pre-existing hypothesis about word order. That is, given the VP-internal subject configuration of underlying word order and language-appropriate setting of the verb raising parameter, postverbal subject word order ensues. Input containing a robust concentration of prosodically unmarked right dislocations of the subject conforms to this order. After all, it is the spoken language that constitutes the vast majority of input to the child. At the very least, the acquisition facts of basic word order show quite clearly that grammaticalization of the proposed type takes place. Even if the developing French grammar were to stop licensing of null and postverbal subjects at some point (which it does not appear to do), it would have passed through a stage in which postverbal subjects were grammaticalized.

Briefly, turning from Modern French as it is spoken to Old French, this analysis appears to be consistent with certain historical facts. According to Adams (1987) and Kroch (1989), among many others, Old French was a verb-second language with null subjects and stressed, nonclitic pronominal subjects. Based on Adams' (1987) account, Middle French lost both pro-drop and the verb-second rule as subject pronouns were cliticized. Prior to cliticization, subject pronouns counted towards satisfying the verb-second requirement. She relates the loss of pro-drop to the loss of verb-second through the notion of canonical government: *pro* in [Spec, IP] was properly governed when the verb raised to Comp. But, under the VP-internal subject hypothesis, canonical or directional government of *pro* in VP-internal subject position holds without verb-raising to Comp. Thus, one can imagine an analysis of the diachronic facts according to which the null subject option was never lost, and the cliticization of subject pronouns was syntactic as well as phonological. In any event, historical observation concurs with the results of research on French acquisition in evidencing an abstract grammatical relationship between subject inversion and *pro*-drop. From the perspective of the typological and functional linguistic literature, it appears that French has undergone relatively little syntactic change. From that perspective, at least, both Old French and contemporary spoken French contain null and postverbal subjects.

7.2 CHANGE AND ACQUISITION IN ENGLISH

This divergence between spoken and written forms when it comes to basic word order is not an issue that arises in the acquisition of English.[9] But there is still something to be learned from comparing where English came from in diachronic terms to where it is now and how it is acquired. The examination here of early English child language suggests that child and adult grammars diverge in a couple of important respects. For one, it was found that the early grammar lacks subject raising in obligatory contexts, namely in negatives and in affirmatives containing auxiliaries. It was also observed that the process of affix lowering which characterizes the adult grammar emerges only after a period of delay. This contrasts with the situation in French, where the initial state or early grammar more closely resembles the target grammar for the spoken language.

In the general approach to acquisition that I assume, one grammatical mechanism may be acquired later than another when it reflects the more marked option or parameter setting. The contrast between French and English in terms of the time course of acquisition thereby suggests that English is more marked than French in the domain of inflectional affixation and, perhaps, that of subject placement. According to diachronic studies, this was not always the case. Middle English was characterized by rich agreement and verb raising to Infl. The positioning of adverbs and negation in Middle English, as well as main verb-subject order in questions, were as found in Modern French. Many theorists associate the leveling of verb inflections with the rise or creation of the category of modal auxiliary verbs (Lightfoot, 1979; Roberts, 1985; Kroch, 1989). On Kroch's (1989) view, the rise of Aux was a reflex of the loss of verb-to-Infl raising, while Roberts (1985) attributes it to the loss of a morphological agreement system. Whatever the causal nature of the relationship, rich agreement and verb raising were closely associated in Middle English. In Modern English, both have been largely replaced by the modal auxiliaries and, in particular, the process of *do*-support.[10]

From the standpoint of acquisition, the changes that took place over the diachronic course of development in English appear to be absolute. Unlike in French, where there is variability in the ordering of subject and verb and where this variability is directly reflected, as I have just argued, in the acquisition process, acquisition provides no clue that English ever allowed main verb raising. With the exception of a small number of errors involving unaccusative verbs, word order errors in which the verb is positioned to the left of the subject are virtually unobserved. That the child acquiring English never postulates verb raising is also confirmed by the lack of errorful productions involving placement of a main verb to the left of a negative, shown in chapter 3.

One aspect of English syntax that has recently generated a certain amount of conflicting opinion is subject raising. Although the VP-internal subject hypothesis is widely accepted, linguists disagree about when the subject in English is actually forced to raise out of the VP and when it is licensed to remain in VP-internal position. Kitagawa (1986) proposed that the underlying order of constituents within the

English VP is subject-final and argued that extraposition is one environment in English where the subject remains unraised at S-structure. Koopman and Sportiche (1988), assuming VP-internal subject-initial order, suggest that English Infl is an obligatory raising category and that the English subjects fail to be assigned nominative Case in VP-internal position. Pesetsky (1989) proposes wh-questions as one exception, reasoning that subject raising to [Spec, IP] is blocked because that position serves as a landing site for matrix wh-movement. Finally, Contreras (1987) claims that — given underlying S-V order within the English VP, affix-lowering, non-barrier status of VP, Infl government and assignment of nominative Case to the subject — there in no reason to postulate subject raising in simple English sentences. To the sentence *John runs* he assigns the D-structure in (11):

(11) $[_{IP}[I[-Past]] [_{VP}[_{NP}John] [_{V'}run]]$

I have adopted Contreras' analysis of English adult grammar in my depiction of English child grammar. If child speech data may be taken as any indication, and I have argued that they can, then subject raising is clearly dispreferred or marked in UG. Why argue, then, that the analysis in (11) is abandoned during the course of acquisition? The position of subjects in affirmatives containing auxiliaries and negatives constitutes a clear exception to this analysis. And, indeed, I have proposed these constructions as prime candidates for the triggering experience that leads the child to reset the parameter responsible for subject raising. But, as Contreras claims, subject raising still may not apply in simple affirmative sentences. Such an approach would have to show that nominative Case assignment under government is blocked when Infl is lexically filled. Along different but instructive lines, Chomsky (1988) argues that Neg serves to block affix-lowering in simple negative sentences.[11] The result is that the only legitimate derivation involves *do*-insertion, as in *John does not run*. Neg and modals may also serve as a barrier to Infl-government of the VP and its specifier, forcing subject raising for Case reasons, contrary to what I suggested earlier for nominative Case assignment in child language.

It is noteworthy in this regard that, in a short-lived intermediate stage between Middle and Modern English, the language contained unemphatic *do* in affirmative declaratives (Kroch, 1989).

While a construction such as *John does run* necessarily involves subject raising, the equivalent sentence without *do*-insertion (*John runs*) does not, on Contreras' (1987) account, necessitate subject raising. It may be, then, that the least effort principle played a role in the disappearance of unemphatic affirmative *do*, similar to the role it appears to play in the marked status of subject raising in the initial state grammar.

These speculations, in which I have tried to show that UG principles of derivational economy may be applied to extinct, adult and child grammars to similar effect, have lead me far afield. My main interest in presenting certain historical facts of English is, once again, for the sake of comparison to French. English diverges from French in the sphere of language change, as it does in acquisition. And it seems that the comparative acquisition data themselves can be used to indicate that certain diachronic changes are absolute changes (i.e. the loss of verb-to-Infl raising in English) and others not (i.e. the loss of inversion and *pro*-drop in French). Presumably the currents of language change will be more visible in the language of the child due a purer manifestation of core principles, before they are partially masked by language-specific, idiosyncratic acquisitions.

NOTES

[1] In more recent writings, Harris speculates that the divergence between spoken and standard French in terms of word order patterns may constitute a relatively stable situation.

[2] It should be noted here, as clarified by Barnes (1985), that terms like *nonstandard French* have generally been used, and specifically in Lambercht (1981), to denote spoken as opposed to written French — and not to refer to a particular dialect. Barnes' own work is based on the study of French that is "spoken by educated people in informal situations".

[3] The examples in (1) and (2) are from Lambrecht (1981), p. 24

[4] The examples in (4) are transcribed adult utterances from Barnes (1985).

5 These examples come from the transcriptions of parental speech in the French database (Suppes, Smith and Leveille, 1973) that is available on the CHILDES system (MacWhinney and Snow, 1985.

6 In addition, one could argue that any perceptual biases of the infant or young child, as in a tendency to attend to phonologically salient elements, would affect learning in this domain.

7 In each case, mother's speech as opposed to father's speech is considered because the mother was the primary caregiver. The analyses described in this section are based on samples of 200–300 utterances from each mother, randomly drawn from the transcribed mother-child interactions.

8 Bear in mind that the two mothers in the Lightbown study are the mother of Daniel and Nathalie.

9 Some have suggested that it may be a live issue with respect to pronouns, claiming that English subject pronouns are undergoing the type of criticization ascribed to French (Givon, 1976; Harris, 1981).

10 See Kroch (1989) for a history of the rise of *do*.

11 Specifically, he suggests that LF-raising of the complex verb [V-Agr-I] across Neg violates the Head Movement Constraint (cf. Chomsky, 1986).

CHAPTER 8

A COMPARATIVE LOOK AT SPANISH ACQUISITION

In this chapter, I survey anecdotal evidence from Spanish child language which, like early French and Italian speech, reveals variability of word order and a strong preference for subject omission. There is some indication that the Spanish child passes through an early phase in which subject-verb order predominates, in contrast to Bates' (1976) findings of a preference for verb-subject order in early Italian and, potentially, in contrast to Contreras' (1987) claim that the ordering of [Spec,VP] and V' in underlying structure is free in Spanish. Overall, however, the pattern of constructions found in early Spanish child language nicely parallels the findings for French and English detailed above.

In a thorough longitudinal study of Spanish developments, Piña (1984) describes the linguistic development of her son Rafael from the start of his acquisition of (Madrid) Spanish as a native language through advanced linguistic stages. Although no statistical information concerning the child's use of various syntactic structures is provided, Piña presents many examples of utterance types according to age, and often mentions which types were used in abundance and which to a lesser extent. From the text, the following points relevant to my concerns here are clear.

8.1 WORD ORDER

At the two-word stage (18–24 months), subject-verb order is utilized more than verb-subject order. Of the 29 utterances produced in the simple present tense and recorded, three contain postverbal subjects, 14 contain nonpronominal preverbal subjects and 12 contain null subjects.[1] Some examples follow in (1) to (3):

(1)   *subject-verb* 18–24 months

      a. nena come (*child eats*)
      b. señor halba (*man talks*)
      c. Rita pega (*Rita hits*)
      d. gafas rompes (*glasses break-2ps*)
      e. autobus anda (*bus goes*)
      f. cabeza duela (*head hurts*)

(2)   *verb-subject* 18–24 months

      a. viene camion (*comes truck*)
      b. anda autobus (*goes bus*)
      c. (me) pega papa (*hits (me) papa*)

(3)   *null subject* 18–24 months

      a. tira (*throws-3ps*)
      b. bajo (*get down-1ps*)
      c. juega (*play-3ps*)

Concerning the examples in (1) through (3), first note the lack of variability in agreement marking on the verb. With only two exceptions, all verbs occur with third person singular (*-3ps*) endings. One exception (1d) involves an agreement error: *gafas* is in the plural (like the English word *glasses*), and thus requires the third person plural (*-3pp*) marking *-en* on the verb. The second exception is (3b), which includes the first person singular (*-1ps*) marking *-o* on the verb. According to the text, certain examples which lack this ending are in fact intended as first person verbal forms. For instance, Piña indicates that the example in (3c) represents an attempt on the part of Rafael at the sentence *(yo) jeugo (I play)*. It should also be noted that two of the postverbal subject constructions in (2) occur with unaccusative verbs, *venir (to come)* and *andar (to go)*. That is, the argument in these constructions is analyzed as being positioned in [VP, NP].

There is corroborating evidence from Gonzales (1970), based on his observation of a small group of Mexican-American children, of infrequent postverbal subjects early on. In his data, the only postverbal subjects at 24 months (the earliest period of observation) occurred with the verb *estar* (locative *to be*). There were few of these, one example being *ahi esta carro* (*there is car*). The remaining verbal utterances at this stage contained null or nonpronominal preverbal subjects. A potential explanation for the dearth of postverbal subjects in the earliest stages of Spanish, in contrast to French, is that, since Spanish fails to mark object agreement on the verb, Spanish may lack the AGR-O node (V. Deprez, personal communication). French participles, on the other hand, are argued to pick up object agreement when they move into AGR-O. While early nonfinite verbs in French may have raised to AGR-O, resulting in the many postverbal subjects in nonfinite clauses observed in chapter 2, Spanish presumably does not have that option. If verb raising to tense is not obligatory in the very early grammar, then untensed verbs in Spanish will only occur with preverbal subjects.

While there is seemingly little variability of word order in the 18–24 month period, Piña describes the 25–30 month period as rich in such variability. Of the many utterances containing postverbal structures at this time, intransitive verb-subject constructions appear to be the most common. Piña notes, further, that many of these contain the reflexive clitic *se*. The examples from the text (p. 263–4) are:

(4)   *verb-subject* 25–30 months

        a. marcho papa (*walked Papa*)

        b. (se) me cae el elefante (*fell to me the elephant*)

        c. no pasa tren (*doesn't pass train*)

        d. se cayo mama (*fell Mama*)

        e. se va tren a la puente (*goes train to the bridge*)

        f. no puede nene (*no can child*)

        g. no ha venido cartero (*no has come the mailman*)

Less common, but still used (in Piña own words), are sentences conforming to V-S-O linear order:[2]

(5)   *verb-subject-object* 25–30 months

    a. cojo papa elefante (*caught Papa the elephant*)
    b. arreglao papa radio (*fixed Papa the radio*)
    c. pega nene oso malo (*hit child bad bear*)
    d. pega el nene elefante (*hit the child elephant*)

Finally, Piña describes the order V-O-S as being less common in comparison to V-S-O. The two examples in the text are:

(6)   *verb-object-subject* 25–30 months

    a. cogiendo papeles yo (*getting papers I*)
    b. coge galletas Rita (*get crackers Rita*)

In examining (4) through (6), note once again that all of the examples in (4), with one exception (4f), occur with unaccusative verbs. Generalizing over (1) and (4), and assuming that Rafael is representative of other children at this stage of grammatical development, one can say that VS constructions in an early stage of Spanish acquisition tend to be unaccusatives, as was found in the case of English child language. However, the examples in (5) and (6) show that the child in the post two-word stage produces postverbal subjects in other constructions, in which the subject is arguably in VP-internal subject position. Within the model of the grammar as it is construed here, (5) and (6) reflect distinct underlying word orders. Assuming that the verb raises to inflection in Spanish, as in French, the V-S-O constructions in (5) result after verb-raising out of a VP with an underlying S-V-O ordering of constituents. Those in (6), in contrast, arise out of an underlying order of V-O-S. Alternatively, they could be produced by rightward movement of the subject and adjunction to VP (Torrego, 1984), whereas V-S-O constructions are only derivable via verb raising.

More data of this type, showing that V-S-O order is more productive in Spanish and emerges earlier than V-O-S, could be viewed as indicative of fixed NP_{subj}-V' ordering within VP in Spanish, where raising of the tensed verb from underlying S-V-O leads to V-S-O. This goes against the hypothesis of underlying V-O-S order in Spanish (cf. Contreras, 1985). Furthermore, it lends support to be claim that postverbal subjects surface only in languages which manifest verb fronting. As for the adult language, some have argued that Spanish has an inherent bias toward V-S-O (Green, 1976).

8.2 NEGATON

I turn to the acquisition of negation in Spanish. The negative particle that expresses simple negation in Spanish, *no*, is clearly not the equivalent of *pas* in French or *not* in English. Rather, it is akin to the negative *ne* in French, and *non* in Italian, occurring as a clitic on the left periphery of the inflectional complex. Verbs that raise to Infl in Spanish and Italian still surface to the right of this particle. However, they occur to the left of other negative elements in tensed structures (Rizzi, 1989):

(7)   French: Jean ne mange plus
         Spanish: Jean no come mas
         Italian: Jean non mangia piu
                   Jean NEG eats more

Piña reports no errors in placement of the negative *no* with respect to the verb. Without exception, Rafael places *no* to the left of the verb. On occasion, however, the negative appears to be absent from utterances intended as negative (e.g. *pasa nada* (*happens nothing*)) intended as *no pasa nada*; and *puede abrir* intended as *no puedo abrir* ((*I*) *cannot open*)). Piña (p. 266) characterizes Rafael's negative utterances at the two-word stage as instantiating the following patterns:

(8)   *two-word stage*

    a. no + object *no caca* (*no caca*)
    b. no + verb *no hay* (*there is no*)
    c. no + verb + object *no hay galletas* (*there is no
       crackers*)
    d. subject + no *yo no* (*not me*)

Note in particular the absence of the pattern subject + no + verb
(+ object) at this stage. Structures conforming to this pattern would be
clear evidence of subject raising. The example in (8d) should most
likely not be interpreted as an instance of subject raising.

In the next stage in the acquisition of negation that Piña describes,
beginning at 26 months, Rafael adds imperative structures with a sentence-initial NP to his negative repertoire:

(9)   *26 to 30 months*

    a. papa, no hables (*papa, don't talk*)
    b. mama, no tires libro (*mama, don't take the book away*)
    c. mama, no duermas mas (*mama, don't sleep anymore*)

These, too, cannot be analyzed as involving subject raising. Clearly, as
revealed by the intonational break, they involve a process of topicalization. Only somewhat later, at about two and a half to there years, do
instantiations of subject + no + verb appear. In (10) are some examples from this older period:

(10)   a. yo no peso mucho (*I don't weigh much*)
    b. eso no vale (*that doesn't count*)
    c. tu no sabes hablar? (*you don't know (how) to talk?*)

8.3 INFLECTIONAL AFFIXATION

If 29 verbal utterances produced and recorded between 18 and 24
months (see above) sound like a surprisingly low number, this is

because the majority of the Rafael's verb-containing utterances during this period were not in the present indicative tense. Piña reports that the earliest verbs used in two-word utterances were tenseless forms. That is, the earliest verbal forms — apparently constituting the majority of forms produced through 22 months — were imperatives, infinitives, past participles and progressive participles, whereas the simple present tense appears to predominate after that:

El *imperativo-desiderativo* fue una de las dos formas verbales mas tempranas... La otra fue el *infinitivo* presentando un indice mas alto de occurencia... Tambien en la etapa de las dos palabras (hasta las 24 mesas) registramos casos con *gerundio*... Y con *participio* ... (p. 245).[3]

Two examples of each type follow in (11) through (14):

(11)   *imperatives*

   a. canta Lola (*sing Lola*)
   b. mama abre (*open Mommy*)

(12)   *infinitives*

   a. nenes senter (*children sit*)
   b. beber argua (*drink water*)

(13)   *progressives*

   a. papa durmiendo (*Papa sleeping*)
   b. hombre hablando (*man speaking*)

(14)   *passive participles*

   a. puerta cerrada (*door closed*)
   b. roto tren (*broken train*)

The utterances in (11) are listed as imperatives by Piña, presumably on the basis of discourse context. As is clear, and as the author notes, the utterances in (13) and (14) are missing the copula (*estar*). For example, (13b) is the child's rendition of *el hombre esta hablando* (*the man is speaking*). Piña further observes that while the earliest verbal clauses reveal knowledge of the distinctions among tenses (i.e. present, imperative, progressive and past), knowledge of agreement early on is barely evident. Piña reports that the earliest marking of person and number occurs at the end of the two-word stage. As support for this claim, Piña notes that most early tensed utterances are specified for third person-singular, resulting in explicit errors of agreement. Consider examples (1d) and (3c) above, as well as (14):

(15)   a. todos quemas (queman)
           (*all burn-2ps*)

        b. puede abrir (no puedo abrir)
           (*I*) (*no*) *can-3ps open*)

At about 24–25 months, Rafael begins to mark agreement more consistently. In Gonzales (1970), in accordance, there is one example of explicit subject-verb agreement at 24 months, e.g. *son pollos* (*are chickens*), while there are many at the subsequent observation (30 months).

I would like to consider the examples in (11) through (14) somewhat further. Recall from the discussion of English child language that progressive participles are base generated verb forms. Emonds (1985) analyzes present participles both in English and in Spanish as base forms (bare VP's). Hyams (1986b) also proposes that V+*ing* forms are lexically, as opposed to syntactically, derived at early stages in English grammar. This approach, which provides an explanation for why the progressive morpheme is first in the order of acquisition of English grammatical morphemes, may also apply to Spanish. This is, in fact, what Emonds (1985) argues for adult Spanish.

Similarly, it might be argued that the passive participles in (14) are lexically derived adjectival participles for the child (cf. Borer and Wexler, 1987). Infinitives, too, may be analyzed as being base generated verbal forms (cf. Emonds, 1985). Finally, note, that the inflectional endings on the *tu* (informal) imperatives in (11) are identical to regular 3ps affixes in the present indicative. All in all, then, an interpretation of the earliest verbs in Spanish as base generated forms that do not necessarily undergo syntactic affixation of inflectional morphology is consistent with findings concerning progressives in English child language and nonfinite forms in French child language. While the Spanish child acquires a complex system of inflectional affixes quite early, we can still discern an initial stage in the grammar of Spanish before the onset of consistent syntactic affixation and, hence, before the onset of consistent verb raising to tense. If this approach is along the right lines, than the early stage of inflexible subject-verb word order may be explained by the absence of obligatory verb raising.

8.4 SUBJECT PRONOUNS

In comparison to English, writes Piña, mastery of the system of personal pronouns in Spanish appears to be somewhat delayed. Piña attributes this to the optionality of subject pronouns in Spanish. The only pronouns to occur at the one-word stage are demonstratives. Some personal forms, both nominative and accusative, are evident during the latter part of the two-word stage (22–25 months), around the time that agreement morphology begins to emerge. The two examples given in the text, apparently the earliest instances of personal subject pronouns, are shown in (16):

(16)   a. yo (voy) a tudia (*I'm going to study*)
        b. abre tu (*open you*)

Note the occurrence of a postverbal subject pronoun in (16b). In contrast to French, subject pronouns in Spanish are strong forms, and thus distribute like lexical subjects. Piña also reports that the subject clitic *se* surges in use at this time. Turning once again to Gonzales (1970) for corroborating evidence, he reports complete absence of subject pronouns at 24 months, although use of reflexive clitics and *se* is well-established at this time. In (17) are some examples from the 24 month stage described in Gonzales:

(17)   a. Juan se va (*Juan leaves*)
         b. me queme (*burnt myself*)
         c. te fuiste, Mami (*you left, Mommy*)

The early acquisition of clitic pronominal forms in Spanish in general accords with the finding that subjects clitics are in early use in French. At the same time, it provides another example from child language of explicit instantiation of a functional projection.

In sum, the course of Spanish development, like that of English and French development, evidences an early stage prior to the mastery of subject raising. If it is true that the child passes through such a stage, as he appears to do based on the findings concerning stages in the acquisition of Spanish negation, then one might analyze early cases of SV order such as those in (1) (prior to productive inflectional affixation) as underived constructions with the subject and verb located within the VP. This clearly holds of the examples with participles and infinitives in (12) through (14). That VS order should fail to be evident at some early stage suggests that it may not be a base generated order. The earliest productive cases of VS order, recall, were unaccusatives (see (2) and (4)), the analysis of which does not necessarily entail, on the basis of liner order of constituents, raising of the verb. Finally, the scarcity of V-O-S constructions in the Spanish child language data also suggests, albeit tentatively, that the order of the verb and the subject within the VP is fixed to underlying S-V order, as in English and perhaps French.

NOTES

[1] This is from Table 15 on p. 246. Pina does not state explicitly that this table, entitled "Formas verbales de los 18 a los 24 mesas" is exhaustive, but this appears to be the case.

[2] In the cases of (5c, d), Ia am deducing that V-S-O, as opposed to V-O-S is the appropriate interpretation.

[3] The English translation of this is:

The imperative-desirative was one of the earliest verbal forms. The other was the infinitive, with a higher index of occurrence. Also at the two-word stage, we note cases to the gerund. And of the (passive) participle.

CHAPTER 9

CONCLUSION

In this book, I have relied on acquisition data to evaluate linguistic-theoretic claims. In particular, I have attempted to provide confirmation of recent proposals in the theoretical literature on the basis of crosslinguistic data from French and English child language. By assuming the VP-internal subject hypothesis, the verb raising analysis of inflectional affixation in French as compared to affix lowering in English, and a principled bias in UG toward isomorphism between levels of representation, a cluster of properties in the early grammar is accounted for.

The abundance of postverbal subjects in French child language is explained on the basis of a combination of syntactic factors. Primarily, on account of the VP-internal subject approach, postverbal subjects in French are construed as unmoved VP-internal subjects. An explanation for the initial absence of subject raising, in terms of the option to assign nominative Case under Infl-government, also sheds light on the endurance of the postverbal subject stage. And the analysis of subject pronouns in French as inflectional clitics further motivates the early grammar to generate postverbal subjects in argument position. The absence of postverbal subjects in English is attributed to the absence of verb raising in that language, and perhaps to a parametric choice of fixed subject-verb order within the VP as well. Contrasting patterns in the acquisition of inflection in French and English, and the related patterns in the placement of negation, were argued to result from the verb raising versus affix lowering processes of inflectional affixation in the two languages. One surprising outcome, however, was the substantial tendency in early English grammar towards auxiliary-initial structures, a tendency strong enough to lead the child to place not only Neg but also *be* in initial position, to the left of the overt subject, in affirmative utterances. Finally, null subjects in English and French child language fall out naturally on the theory that they are VP-internal subjects, directionally governed by Infl.

At the same time, the evidence of syntactically principled behavior in French and English acquisition should be taken as support for recent developments in syntactic theory, especially for the VP-internal subject hypothesis. English findings on word order are consistent with the unaccusative analysis of select verbs. French findings on word order strongly support the VP-internal subject approach. Recall, as I have argued, that negation in child language cannot be construed as an extrasyntactic phenomenon, but can only be reasonably interpreted when Neg is analyzed as residing under Infl. The comparative results on inflection and negation indicate that the parametric distinction between English and French grammar, wherein only French has main verb raising, indeed holds and is indeed an early acquisition. And the comparative findings on children's analyses of subject pronouns suggest that French subject clitics are generated in Infl, as some linguists have claimed.

In concluding, I want to comment on an established approach to early grammar, one that has a long history in the study of child language. This is the idea that child language lacks functional categories. Early versions of this generalization, as in the work of Roger Brown (Brown and Fraser, 1963), simply describe pre-school utterances as lacking closed class elements. This fact has sometimes been interpreted as the result of output limitations, or of filtering out prosodically nonsalient items. But many have also argued that it reflects the nature of the child's grammatical representations (e.g. Pinker, 1984). One recent form that this outlook takes is the proposal that child language is best characterized by the absence of Infl, or of all functional projections, at early stages (Guilfoyle and Noonan, 1988; Kazman, 1988; Aldridge, 1988; Radford, 1990). According to Guilfoyle and Noonan, for example, functional tree structure matures as a whole sometime after the second birthday. Before that time, children are said to represent only lexical categories. They are presumably unable to inflect verbs or assign nominative Case to the subject. Bloom (1988) and Lebeaux (1988) also present arguments to the effect that the case filter is not operational in the early grammar.

As mentioned earlier, one difficult problem for the theory that inflection is simply absent from two year-old grammar is the fact that complex inflectional paradigms are in place very early in the child learning, for example, Polish (Weist *et al.* 1984) or Italian (Bates, 1976; Hyams, 1984). And the kind of data I have presented in this book give rise to additional problems for the view the Case filter and functional projections undergo maturation, are absent at some early stage, or are otherwise dispensable in the analysis of early child grammar. Without appealing to the young French-speaking child's knowledge or representation of Infl, for example, there would be no way to capture the generalizations that verbs are positioned according to inflectional features, and that negation and subject clitics pattern precisely as a function of verb movement. Such findings result from careful analysis of the data and demonstrate the active role that functional projections play in child grammar. With respect to Infl, at least, they suggest that it is the nature of the derivational system in conjunction with certain delays in derivational acquisition that give rise to the appearance of there being an inflectional system in the very early grammar.

The pared down form of English child utterances is deceptive, their lexical deficiencies masking complex grammatical representations. This is by no means a new insight. What is new is the use of a comparative framework to point out where superficial analyses of child utterances may be lacking. As crosslinguistic studies go, this has been a fairly unambitious undertaking. But I hope that, in demonstrating how child grammars may be profitably compared, it inspires further study of acquisition from a comparative perspective.

REFERENCES

Adams, M. 1987. From Old French to the theory of pro-drop. *Natural Language and Linguistic Theory* 5: 1–32.

Akmajian, A., Demers, R. & Harnish, R. 1984. *Linguistics: an introduction to language and communication* (2nd edit.). Cambridge MA: MIT Press.

Aldridge, M. 1988. The acquisition of INFL. *Research Monographs in Linguistics.* Bangor: UCNW.

Ashby, W. 1988. The syntax, pragmatics, and sociolinguistics of left- and right-dislocation in French. *Lingua* 75: 203–229.

Bailard, J. 1982. Le francais de deamin: VSO ou VOS? In A. Ahlqvist (ed.) *Papers from the 5th international conference on historical linguistics,* 20–28. Amsterdam: Benjamins.

Baker, M. 1988. *Incorporation.* Chicago: University of Chicago Press.

Barnes, B. 1985. *The pragmatics of left detachment in spoken Standard French.* Amsterdam: Benjamins.

Barnes, B. 1986. An empirical study of the syntax and pragmatics of left dislocations in spoken French. In O. Jaeggli & C. Silva-Corvalan (eds.) *Studies in Romance linguistics.* Dordrecht: Foris.

Bates, E. 1976. *Language and context: studies in the acquisition of pragmatics.* New York: Academic Press.

Belletti, A. 1982. Morphological passive and pro-drop. *Journal of Linguistic Research* 2.

Belletti, A. 1988. The case of unaccusatives. *Linguistic Inquiry* 19.

Bellugi, U. 1967. *The acquisition of negation.* Doctoral dissertation, Harvard University.

Bever, T. G. 1970. The cognitive basis for linguistic structures. In J. R. Hayes (ed.) *Cognition and the development of language.* New York: Wiley.

Bloch, O. 1924. La phrase dans le langage de l'enfant. *Journal de Psychologie* 21: 18–43.

Bloom, L. 1970. *Language development: form and function in emerging grammars.* Cambridge MA: MIT Press.

Bloom, P. 1988. *Subject position and child language.* ms.

Bloom. P. 1989. Why do children omit subjects? *Papers and Reports on Child Language Development.* Stanford University, Department of Linguistics.

Bonet, E. 1989. *Postverbal subjects in Catalan.* ms.

Borer, H. 1984. *Parametric syntax: case studies in Semitic and Romance languages.* Dordrecht: Foris.

Borer, H. 1986a. I-Subjects. *Linguistic Inquiry* 17.

Borer, H. (ed.) 1986b. *The syntax of pronominal clitics*. New York: Academic Press.

Borer, H. 1989. Anaphoric AGR. In O. Jaeggli & K. Safir (eds.).

Borer, H & Wexler, K. 1987 The maturation of syntax. In T. Roeper & E. Williams (eds.), 123–172.

Borer, H. & Wexler, K. 1988. *The maturation of grammatical principles*. ms.

Bowerman, M. 1973. *Early syntactic development*. London: Cambridge University Press.

Bowerman, M. 1982. Reorganizational processes in lexical and syntactic development. In E. Wanner and L. Gleitman (eds.).

Brandi, L & Cordin, P. 1989. Two Italian dialects and the null subject parameter. In O. Jaeggli & K. Safir (eds.).

Braine, M. 1963. The ontogeny of English phrase structure: the first phase. *Language* 39: 1–13.

Braine, M. 1976. Children's first word combinations. *Monographs of the Society for Research in Child Development* 41,1.

Brown, R. 1973. *A first language: the early stages*. Cambridge MA: Harvard University Press.

Brown, R. & Bellugi, U. 1964. Three processes in the child's acquisition of syntax. *Harvard Educational Review* 34: 133–151.

Brown, R. & Fraser, C. 1963. The acquisition of syntax. In C. Cofer & B. Musgrave (eds.) *Verbal behavior and learning: problems and principles*. New York: McGraw Hill: 115–201.

Burzio, L. 1986. *Italian syntax*. Dordrecht: Reidel.

Campbell, R. 1991. Paper presented at Glow, Leiden.

Champaud, 1988. On-line documentation. CHILDES.

Chien, Y. -C. & Lust, B. 1985. The concepts of subject and topic in first language acquisition of Mandarin Chinese. *Child Development*.

Chomsky, N. 1981 *Lectures on government and binding*. Dordrecht: Foris.

Chomsky, N. 1986a. *Knowledge of language: its nature, origin and use*. New York: Praeger.

Chomsky, N. 1986b. *Barriers*. Cambridge MA: MIT Press.

Chomsky, N. 1988. *Some notes on economy of derivation and representation*. ms.

Clark, E. 1985. The acquisition of Romance with special reference to French. In D. Slobin (ed.).

Contreras, H. 1985. Spanish bare NPs and the ECP. In I. Bordelois, H. Contreras and K. Zagona (eds.) *Generative studies in Spanish syntax*. Dordrecht: Foris.

Contreras, H. 1987. Small clauses in English and Spanish. *Natural Language and Linguistic Theory* 5: 225–243.

Deprez, V. 1988. Stylistic inversion and verb movement. ESCOL Proceedings.

Deprez, V. 1989. *On the typology of syntactic positions and the nature of chains*. Doctoral dissertation, MIT.

Deprez, V. 1990. On two ways of moving the verb in French. *MIT Working Papers* 12.

Deprez V. & Pierce, A. in press. Negation and functional projections in early grammar. *Linguistic Inquiry.*

de Villiers, J. & de Villiers, P. 1973. A cross-sectional study of the acquisition of grammatical morphemes in child speech. *Journal of Psycholinguistic Research* 2: 267–278.

de Villiers, J. & de Villiers, P. 1979. Form and function in the development of sentence negation. *Papers and Reports on Child Language Development* 17: 56–64. Stanford University, Department of Linguistics.

de Villiers, J. & de Villiers, P. 1985. The acquisition of English. In D. Slobin (ed.).

Dietiker, S. 1978. *En bonne forme: revision de grammaire francaise.* Lexington: D. C. Heath and Company.

Emonds, J. 1976. *A transformational approach to English syntax.* New York: Academic Press.

Emonds, J. 1978. The verbal complex V'-V in French. *Linguistic Inquiry* 9.

Emonds, J. 1985. *A unified theory of syntactic categories.* Dordrecht: Foris.

Fabb, N. 1984. *Syntactic affixation.* Doctoral dissertation, MIT.

Feldman, H., Goldin-Meadow, S. & Gleitman, L. R. 1978. Beyond Herodotus: the creation of language by linguistically deprived deaf children. In A. Lock (ed.) *Action, symbol and gesture: the emergence of language.* New York: Academic Press.

Felix, S. 1987. *Cognition and language growth.* Dordrecht: Foris.

Francois, D. 1974. *Francais parle: analyse des unites phonetique et significatives d'un corpus recueilli dans la region parisienne.* S.E.L.A.F.

Fukui, N. 1988. Deriving the differences between English and Japanese: a case study in parametric syntax. *English Linguistics* 5: 249–270.

Fukui, N. & Speas, M. 1987. *Specifiers and projections.* ms. MIT.

Givon, T. 1976. Topic, pronoun and grammatical agreement. In. C. Li (ed.) *Subject and topic.* New York: Academic Press.

Gleitman, L., Gleitman, H., Landau, B. & Wanner, E. 1988. Where learning begins: initial representations for language learning. In F. Newmeyer (ed.) *Language: psychological and biological aspects.* London: Cambridge University Press.

Gleitman, L. & Wanner E. 1982. *Language acquisition: the state of the art.* London: Cambridge University Press.

Gleitman, L. & Wanner, E. 1982. Language acquisition: the state of the art. In L. Gleitman and E. Wanner (eds.).

Gilligan, G. M. 1987. *A crosslinguistic approach to the pro-drop parameter.* Doctoral dissertation, University of Southern California.

Gonzalez, G. 1970. *The acquisition of Spanish grammar by native Spanish speakers.* Doctoral dissertation, University of Texas.

Grimshaw, J. 1987. Unaccusatives — an overview. *Proceedings of the Northeastern Linguistic Society* 17, 244–258.

Green, J. 1976. How free is word order in Spanish? In M. Harris (ed.).

Greenfield, P. & Smith, J. 1976. *The structure of communication in early language development.* New York: Academic Press.

Gruber, J. 1967. Topicalization in child language. *Foundations of Language* 3: 37–65.

Guilfoyle, E. 1984. *The acquisition of tense and the emergence of lexical subjects in child grammars of English*. McGill Working Papers in Linguistics.

Guilfoyle, E. & Noonan, M. 1988. *Functional categories and language acquisition*. Paper presented at the Thirteenth Annual Boston University Conference on Language Development.

Guillaume, P. 1927. Les debuts de la phrase dans le langage de l'enfant. *Journal de Psychologie* 24: 1–25. English translation by E. Clark in C. Ferguson & D. Slobin (eds.) 1973 *Studies of child language development*. New York: Holt, Rinehart and Winston.

Harman, E. & Montagnes, I. (eds.) 1976. *The thesis and the book*. Toronto: University of Toronto Press.

Harris, M. 1976. A typological approach to word order change in French. In M. Harris (ed.) *Romance syntax: synchronic and diachronic perspectives*. Salford: University of Salford Press.

Harris, M. 1978. *The evolution of French syntax*. London: Longman.

Harris, M. 1981. It's I, it's me: further reflections. *Studia Anglica Posnaniensia*, 13: 17–20.

Higginson, R. 1985. *Fixing: a demonstration of the child's active role in language acquisition*. Doctoral dissertation, Washington State University.

Huang, J. 1984. On the distribution and reference of empty pronouns. *Linguistic Inquiry* 15: 531–574.

Huang, J. 1989. Pro-drop in Chinese: a generalized control theory. In O. Jaeggli & K. Safir (eds.).

Hyams, N. 1984. Semantically-based child grammars: some empirical inadequacies. *Papers and Reports on Child Language Development*. Stanford University, Department of Linguistics.

Hyams, N. 1986a. *Language acquisition and the theory of parameters*. Dordrecht: Reidel.

Hyams, N. 1986b. *The core/periphery distinction and the acquisition of inflection*. Paper presented at the Eleventh Annual Boston University Conference on Language Development.

Hyams, N. 1986c. The interpretation and acquisition of Italian impersonal si. In H. Borer (ed.).

Hyams, N. & Jaeggli, O. 1988. *Null subjects and morphological development in child language*. ms.

Jaeggli, O. 1982. *Topics in Romance syntax*. Dordrecht: Foris.

Jaeggli, O. 1986a. Three issues in the theory of clitics: case, doubled NPs and extraction. In H. Borer (ed.).

Jaeggli, O. 1986b. Passive. *Linguistic Inquiry* 19.

Jaeggli, O & Safir, K. 1989. The null subject parameter and parametric theory. In O. Jaeggli & K. Safir (eds.).

Jaeggli, O. & Safir, K. (eds.) 1989. *The null subject parameter*. Dordrecht: Kluwer.

Jaeggli, O. & Silva-Corvalan, C. (eds.). 1986. *Studies in Romance linguistics*. Dordrecht: Foris.

Kayne, R. 1975. *French syntax*. Cambridge MA: MIT Press.

Kayne, R. 1984. *Connectedness and binary branching*. Dordrecht: Foris.

Kayne, R. 1987. *Facets of Romance past participle agreement*. ms.

Kayne, R. 1989. Null subjects and clitic climbing. In O. Jaeggli & K. Safir (eds.), 239–261.

Kazman, R. 1988. *Null arguments and the acquisition of Case and INFL*. Paper presented at the Thirteenth Annual Boston University Conference on Language Development.

Kazman, R. 1990. *The genesis of functional categories*. Paper presented at the Fifteenth Annual Boston University Conference on Language Development.

Kitagawa, Y. 1986. *Subjects in Japanese and English*. Doctoral dissertation, University of Massachusetts.

Klima, E. & Bellugi, U. 1966. Syntactic regularities in the speech of children. In J. Lyons & R. Wales *Psycholinguistic papers*. Edinburgh: Edinburgh University Press, 183–208.

Koopman, H. & Sportiche, D. 1988. *Subjects*. ms.

Kratzer, A. 1989. *Stage-level and individual-level predicates*. ms.

Kroch, A. 1989. Reflexes of grammar in patterns of language change. *Language Variation and Change* 1: 199–244.

Kuroda, Y. 1986. *Whether we agree or not*. ms.

Laka, I. 1989. Constraints on sentence negation. *MIT Working Papers in Linguistics* 10.

Lambrecht, K. 1981. *Topic, antitopic and verb agreement in non-standard French*. Amsterdam: Benjamins.

Larsson, E. 1979. La dislocation en francais: etude de syntax generative. *Etudes Romanes de Lund* 28. Lund: Gleerup.

Lasnik, H. 1989. *Case and expletives: towards a parametric account*. Paper presented at the Second Princeton Workshop on Comparative Grammar.

Lebeaux, D. 1987. Comments on Hyams. In T. Roeper & E. Williams (eds.).

Lebeaux, D. 1988. *Language acquisition and the form of the grammar*. Doctoral dissertation, University of Massachusetts.

Li, A. 1985. *Abstract case in chinese*. Doctoral dissertation, University of Southern California.

Lightbown, P. 1977. *Consistency and variation in the acquisition of French*. Doctoral dissertation, Columbia University.

Lightfoot, D. 1979. *The principles of diachronic syntax*. Cambridge: Cambridge University Press.

Lightfoot, D. 1988. Syntactic change. In F. Newmeyer (ed.) *Linguistics: the Cambridge survey*. Cambridge: Cambridge University Press.

Lightfoot, D. 1991. *How to set parameters: arguments from language change.*

Cambridge MA: MIT Press.

Lust, B. 1977. Conjunction reduction in child language. *Journal of Child Language* 4: 257–288.

Lust, B. & Mervis, C. 1980. Development of coordination in the natural speech of young children. *Journal of Child Language* 7: 279–304.

MacWhinney, B. & Snow, C. 1985. The child language data exchange system. *Journal of Child Language* 12.

McNeill, D. 1970. *The acquisition of language.* New York: Harper and Row.

Newport, E., L. Gleitman & Gleitman, H. 1977. Mother, I'd rather do it myself: some effects and non-effects of maternal speech style. In C. Snow and C. Ferguson (eds.) *Talking to children: language input and acquisition.* Cambridge: Cambridge University Press.

Perlmutter, D. 1978. Impersonal passives and the unaccusative Hypothesis. *Proceedings of the Berkeley Linguistics Society* 4: 157–189.

Pesetsky, D. 1989. *Language-particular processes and the earliness principle.* ms.

Peters, A. 1983. *The units of language acquisition.* London: Cambridge University Press.

Pierce, A. 1987. *Null subjects in the acquisition of French.* Paper presented at the Twelfth Annual Boston University Conference on Language Development.

Pierce, A. 1989. *On the emergence of syntax: a crosslinguistic study.* Doctoral dissertation, MIT.

Pierce, A. & Deprez, V. 1990. *A crosslinguistic study of negation in early syntactic development.* Paper presented at the Fifteenth Annual Conference on Language Development, Boston University, October 19–21.

Piña, F. H. 1984. *Teorias psico-sociolinguisticos y su aplicacion a la adquisicion del espanol como lengua materna.* Madrid: Siglo XXI.

Pinker, S. 1984. *Language learnability and language development.* Cambridge MA: Harvard University Press.

Pinker, S. 1986. Productivity and conservatism in language acquisition. In W. Demopoulos & A. Marras (eds.) *Language learning and concept acquisition.* *Norwood: Ablex.*

Platzack, C. 1990. *A grammar without functional categories: A syntactic study of early Swedish Child language,* Unpublished ms.

Pollock, J-Y. 1989. Verb movement, universal grammar, and the structure of IP. *Linguistic Inquiry* 20: 365–424.

Pye, C. 1983. Mayan telegraphese: intonational determinants of inflectional development in Quiche Mayan. *Language* 59.

Radford, A. 1990. *Syntactic theory and the acquisition of English syntax.* Oxford: Basil Blackwell.

Ramer, A. 1976. Syntactic styles in emerging language. *Journal of Child Language* 3: 49–62.

Raposo, E. 1987. Case theory and INFL-to-COMP: the inflected infinitive in European Portuguese. *Linguistic Inquiry* 18: 85–109.

Read, C. & Schreiber, P. 1982. Why short subjects are harder to find than long ones. In L. Gleitman and E. Wanner (eds.).

Rizzi, L. 1982. *Issues in Italian syntax*. Dordrecht: Foris.

Rizzi, L. 1986a. Null objects in Italian and the theory of pro. *Linguistic Inquiry* 17: 501–557.

Rizzi, L. 1986b. On the status of subject clitics in Romance. In O. Jaeggli & C. Silva-Corvalan (eds.)

Rizzi, L. 1989. *Relativized minimality*. Paper presented at the Second Princeton Workshop on Comparative Grammar.

Rizzi, L. & Roberts, I. 1989 *French complex inversion*. ms.

Roeper, T. 1973. Connecting children's language and linguistic theory. In T. Moore (ed.).

Roeper, T. & Williams, E. (eds.) 1987. *Parameter setting*. Dordrecht: Reidel.

Roberts, I. 1985. Agreement parameters and the development of English modal auxiliaries. *Natural Language and Linguistic Inquiry* 3: 21–58.

Rosen, C. 1989. Unpublished ms. Brandeis University.

Rouveret, A. & Vergnaud, J. -R. 1980. Specifying reference to the subject. *Linguistic Inquiry* 11: 97–202.

Sabeau-Jouannet, E. 1975. Les premiers acquisitions syntaxiques chez les enfants français unilangues. *La Linguistique* 11: 105–122.

Sachs, J. 1983. Talking about the, there and then: the emergence of displaced reference in parent-child discourse. In K. E. Nelson (ed.) *Children's language* Vol. 4. Hillsdale: Erlbaum.

Safir, K. 1986. Subject clitics and the NOM-drop parameter. In H. Borer (ed.) *The syntax of pronominal clitics*. Orlando: Academic Press, 333–356.

Shipley, E., Smith, C. & Gleitman, L. 1969. A study in the acquisition of language: free responses to commands. In *Language* 45: 322–42.

Sinclair, H. 1973. Language acquisition and cognitive development. In T. Moore (ed.).

Sinclair, H. & Bronkart J. 1972. SVO – a linguistic universal? A study in developmental psycholinguistics. *Journal of Experimental Child Psychology* 14, 329–348.

Slobin, D. (ed.) 1985. *The crosslinguistic study of language acquisition* Vol. 1. Hillsdale: Erlbaum.

Smith, N. 1973. *The acquisition of phonology*. Cambridge: Cambridge University Press.

Sportiche, D. 1988. A theory of floating quantifiers and its corollaries for constituent structure. *Linguistic Inquiry* 19: 425–449.

Stowell, T. 1978. What was there before there was there. In D. Farkas *et al.* (eds.) *Papers from the fourteenth regional meeting*, Chicago Linguistics Society, 457–471.

Stowell, T. 1983. Subjects across categories. *The Linguistic Review* 2: 285–312.

Stromswold, K. 1990. *Learnability and the acquisition of auxiliaries*. Doctoral dissertation, MIT.

Suppes, P., Smith, R. & Leveille, M. 1973. The French syntax of a child's noun phrases. *Archives de Psychologie* 42.

Torrego, E. 1984. On inversion in Spanish and some of its effects. *Linguistic Inquiry* 15.

Travis, L. 1984. *Parameters and effects of word order variations.* Doctoral dissertation, MIT.

Valian, V. 1989. Children's production of subjects: competence, performance, and the null subject parameter. *Papers and Reports on Child Language Development.* Stanford University, Department of Linguistics.

Vickner, S. 1990. *Verb movement and the licensing of NP-positions in the Germanic languages.* Doctoral dissertation, University of Geneva.

Vickner, S. & Schwartz, B. 1988. All verb second clauses are CPs. *Working Papers in Scandanavian Syntax* 43: 27–50.

Vygotsky, L. 1962 *Thought and language.* Cambridge MA: MIT press.

Wanner, E. & Gleitman, L. 1982. *Language acquisition: the state of the art.* Cambridge: Cambridge University Press.

Weissenborn, J. 1988a. *The acquisition of clitic object pronouns and word order in French: syntax or morphology?* ms.

Weissenborn, J. 1988b. *Null subjects in early grammars: implications for parameter-setting theories.* Paper presented at the Thirteenth Annual Boston University Conference on Language Development.

Weissenborn, J. & Verrips, M. 1989. *Negation as a window to the structure of early child language.* ms.

Weist, R., Wysocka, H., Witkowska-Stadnik, K, Buczowska, E., & Konieczna E. 1984. The defective tense hypothesis: on the emergence of tense and aspect in child Polish. *Journal of Child Language* 11: 347–374.

Williams, E. (1990) *Theta-theory in syntax* in preparation, MIT Press

Wode, H. 1977. Four early stages in the development of L1 negation. *Journal of Child Language* 4: 87–102.

Zanuttini, R. 1989. Two types of negative markers. *Proceedings of the Northeastern Linguistic Society*, 20.

Zubizarreta, M. L. 1985. The relation between morphophonology and morphosyntax: the case of Romance causatives. *Linguistic Inquiry* 16, 247–289.

INDEX OF NAMES

INDEX OF SUBJECTS